D1243032

SACRED
SECRETS

SACRED
SECRETS

THE SANCTITY OF SEX IN
JEWISH LAW AND LORE

GERSHON WINKLER

JASON ARONSON INC.
Northvale, New Jersey
Jerusalem

This book was set in 12 pt. Souvenir by Alpha Graphics of Pittsfield, New Hampshire.

10 9 8 7 6 5 4 3 2 1

Library of Congress Cataloging-in-Publication Data

Winkler, Gershon, 1949–
    Sacred secrets : the sanctity of sex in Jewish law and lore / by
Gershon Winkler.
        p.   cm.
    Includes bibliographical references and index.
    ISBN 0-7657-9974-X (alk. paper)
    1. Sex in rabbinical literature.   2. Sex in the Bible.   3. Sex—
Religious aspects—Judaism.   4. Rabbinical literature—History and
criticism.   I. Title.
BM496.9.S48W56   1998
296.3'66—dc21   97-19872

Manufactured in the United States of America. Jason Aronson Inc. offers books and cassettes. For information and catalog write to Jason Aronson Inc., 230 Livingston Street, Northvale, New Jersey 07647.

Contents

CONTENTS

1
JUDEO LIBIDO

Unlike the common cold, which has been with us for many thousands of years, sexual taboo is a disease invented by humans and blamed on God. By this era it has germinated into a source of emotional and physical conflict so severe as to warrant the unprecedented emergence of physicians and counselors specializing in human sexual inadequacies. So, taboo or not taboo? That is the question that both Jews and Christians must ask of their current religious sex ethic. For Jews it is a code of ethics that is anything but Jewish, and for Christians it is a moral structure founded upon blatant misinterpretation of Jewish Scriptures.

Most of us are passive beneficiaries of so-called Western civilization, accustomed to a code of sexual ethics we glibly call "Judeo-Christian," a code that is essentially far more Christian than it is Judeo. Judaism absorbed much of sexual taboo only after centuries of subjection to host religions and cultures that all but squelched the notion of sensuality, often by pain of death. Under such conditions, laws evolved in the Jewish codes that strove to parallel the sexual ethics of Jews with those of Christians, for example, so that the Jewish community would hold yet one more ace in its survival cards. Women, Jewish and Christian alike, often were chosen as well, as fodder for the fires of hatred sparked by a religion of love. After all, the medieval church barred women from the use of their intellect, intuition, or medicinal knowledge, the exercise of which would taint them instantly with suspicions of sorcery and witchcraft, with consequences of torture and death. No wonder the Jewish communities, persecuted always for theological reasons, kept their people in check during those many centuries of subjection to Church rule. And while Jewish women enjoyed respect as spiritual teachers, their learning and public positions in the Jewish communities of Christian Europe were subdued and discouraged over the centuries in order to protect them from the bonfires of misogyny that burned randomly about them. Were Jewish women to become too public, were the sexual ethics of the Jews to become less stringent than those of the Church, it would only further fuel the inferno that consumed them unceasingly for close to 1,700 years. They couldn't take such chances, so the ancient laws that permitted polygamy, variations in positions during sex, coitus interruptus, nonmarital sex, contraception, etc., were gradually sublimated, gathering the dust of ages while hidden away in tiny print along the margins of ancient and medieval texts preserved for posterity.

Nonetheless, the mystery of how sex became stigmatized and turned into something evil and dirty to begin with remains at large. The eighteenth-century Rabbi Yaakov of Emden tackled the question in regards to his own people and posits that the Jews' 1,700-year-old subjection to the strictures of the Church had obviously supplanted their original Judaic sex ethics with those of Christianity (*Shaylot Ya'avetz*, vol. 2, no. 15 toward end). Emden's theory is somewhat echoed by the noted Anglican theologian, Dr. Derrick S. Bailey:

> The Christian attitude to sexuality in all its aspects was profoundly affected by the ascendancy of Hellenistic dualism over Hebraic naturalism during the first great age of the Church. The Jewish conceptions of coitus, marriage, and children, positive and affirmative within their inevitable limits, were almost entirely overlaid by the Graeco-Oriental tendency to . . . look upon sexuality as something not only emotionally disturbing, but also in some sense defiling and tainted with evil. (*Sexual Relations in Christian Thought* [New York: Harper & Bros., 1959], pp. 100–101)

Sure enough, as one examines the earliest Jewish teachings of other aspects of human sexual dynamics, it becomes increasingly clear that somewhere between the "Judeo" and the "Christian" some very basic concepts about sex got carelessly, if not deliberately, distorted. One theory has it that Paul, not Jesus, was responsible for setting this trend into motion and that he was motivated to downplay sensuality because he believed that the physical world was coming to an end and that the "second coming" was at hand. But regardless of who was to blame, the fact remains that this mythical "Judeo-Christian" sex ethic has left countless dangling helplessly between the puritan values with which they have been raised and the redefined moral structures now being pressed upon them by a new paradigm. The re-examination of the original Judaic sources on sex is therefore extremely urgent, for both Jews and Christians alike (as well as for non-religiously affiliated members of Western society), for both suffer their psychosexual ailments on account of a moralistic system intended for neither.

The primary Judaic view on sex is best summarized by the thirteenth-century Rabbi Moshe ben Nachmon (*Ramban*) in his classical sex manual, *Iggeret HaKodesh*, or "Epistle of Holiness" (p. 175):

No one should claim that sex is ugly or repulsive. God forbid! For sexual intercourse is called "knowing" in the Scriptures (Gen. 4:1), and not in vain is it called thus. . . . If we were to say that sex is repulsive, then we blaspheme God Who created the genitals. . . . All body parts are neutral; the use we make of them determines whether they are holy or unholy.

During the same century that Rabbi Moshe ben Nachmon wrote these words, Pope Innocent III declared that "the sexual act is so shameful as to be inherently wicked." Less extreme Christian expositors of the same era warned their constituents that "the holy spirit absented Himself from the room of married folk performing the act even for generation alone" (*What Modern Catholics Think About Birth Control* [Signet, 1964], p. 54)—a view diametrically opposed to the tradition by which Jesus himself was raised: "When a man and a woman unite with mutual love and desire, the Divine Presence *abides* with them" (Babylonian Talmud, *Sotah* 17a). The Church also advocated sexual abstinence during special feast days and the holy season, whereas Judaism *encouraged* sexual relations *especially* during the holy Sabbath and the sacred seasons (Babylonian Talmud, *Kesuvot* 62b; *Zohar B'reishet* 35:130). On the contrary, the Judaic perspective envisioned the sex act as "worthy, good, and beneficial even to the soul. No other human activity can compare with it. . . . There is nothing impure or defective about it, rather there is much elation" (Rabbi Yaakov Emden in *Mor Uk'tziah*, no. 240).

It comes as no surprise, therefore, that both the Jerusalem and Babylonian Talmuds, the most authoritative post-biblical bodies of ancient Judaic law, ethics, and philosophy, discuss sex and nudity with the same ease and comfort with which they discuss prayer and angels. In the middle of an exposition on the laws of the Sabbath, for example, the Talmud records the third-century Rabbi Chisda's sexual counsel to his daughters:

> When your husband engages you in foreplay, to arouse your passions toward intercourse, and he reaches for your breasts with one hand and for the vaginal opening with the other, allow your breasts to be caressed so that your desire be aroused, but as for your vagina, do not make it accessible to him right away, in order to increase his passions by teasing him. (Babylonian Talmud, *Shabbat* 140b, based on the rendition of the eleventh-century Rabbi Shlomo Yitchaki [*Rashi*])

Rabbi Chisda counseling his daughters in sexual matters was certainly not an isolated case in these ancient writings. According to the twelfth-century mystic Rabbi Yehudah the Pious, couples seeking advice concerning sexual technique and dysfunction frequently called upon the rabbis of yesteryear (*Sefer Chasidim,* no. 1118). The sex act, it is apparent, was not at all looked upon as a strictly procreative, duty-oriented function, but rather as a legitimate and healthy activity even for pleasure alone. They cautioned only that, as wonderful and wholesome as it is, the sexual impulse needs to be handled with care.

The Talmud, for example, employs a great many parables about sexual lust to illustrate the enormity of this very basic instinct that is at the core of as much upheaval as bliss. The very strict, unbending laws about adultery, for instance, common to virtually all religions and cultures, are most probably due to the immense chaos that can result from unrestricted sexual license. If everyone had sex with anyone— assuming there was mutual consent, of course—there would be bloodshed beyond imagination as jealous, possessive men *and* women would be at each other's throats in vengeance over each having slept with the other's partner.

Possessiveness of a mate is surely to be found in both genders, but because men have been programmed through the ages to be the chiefs of their households and the initiators of matrimony, it follows that they could have more than one woman partner while their wives could not—not so much because of a patriarchic double standard, but because they are into ownership, be it of property or wives, whereas women were programmed through the ages to "go along" with the flow of societal and cultural direction ordained by men. Whether this state of things is right or wrong is irrelevant to the fact of life that this is how it has been for ages and continues to be to this day. Western society is far more tolerant, for example, of a man who is sexually involved with a number of women than it is of a woman who is sexually involved with more than one man. American law might sound hoity-toity in its self-righteous ban on polygamy, yet American culture is replete with married men who engage sexually with women other than their wives. And while adultery among women is climbing at this writing to meet the statistics of adultery among men, the way society looks at it is still entangled in the double standard, which is: tolerated for men, unacceptable for women.

Jewish law is at least not hypocritical on this issue. A married man does not commit adultery by having sex with a woman other than his wife, as long as the second woman is not married to anyone else. He even may marry several wives at one time, as long as he can provide sexual gratification, food, and shelter for each of them accordingly (Babylonian Talmud, *Yevamot* 65; *Mishnah Torah, Hilchot Ishut* 14:3; *Ramban ahl ha-Torah* on Exod. 21:11). A married woman, however, commits adultery if she has sex with a man other than her husband, while a single woman commits no wrong if she has sex with a man, whether he is married or single. It boils down to this: Once you commit yourself to the patriarchic design of what we call "marriage," then you are bound by rules that obviously favor men, rules that are liberal for them and restrictive for women. Religious folk of course will claim that it is God's will that it be so, but such claims are only as divine as the people who swear by them. What God wills and what mortal male prophets purport to be God's will are not always the same. The Jewish tradition is full of stories about how the prophet got it wrong, about the discrepancy between God and religion (the theme of my book *The Place Where You Are Standing is Holy*).

The nineteenth-century Rabbi Shmuel Dovid Luzatto of Italy writes how the sexual restrictions delineated in the Torah are not to be mistaken as part of what we call "religious" laws but are rather *societal* laws instituted for the people, as they were then becoming a nation. Every society evolves its rules for those who wish to be a part of it, rules designed primarily to keep law and order, to prevent violence, to promote stability in the nation, and, of course, to further a particular agenda. These laws are brilliantly created by the societal leaders, who mostly try their best to imbue their new community or society with a sense of peacefulness and purposefulness. It doesn't always work, of course. The Founding Fathers of the United States instituted the law of liberty for all, while their own estates were swarming with slaves.

Many of the Mosaic prohibitions created so many incidents of war and havoc among the Jewish tribes themselves that most of these laws eventually had to get reinterpreted so that zealots wouldn't take them so literally. A little more than a thousand years after the period of Moses, teachers down the ages had so thoroughly reinterpreted the laws that he had transcribed "from the lips of God" that it was virtually impossible to execute someone for a capital offense. Moreover, capital offenses such as that of the rebellious son were thrown out of the books altogether (Babylonian Talmud, *Sanhedrin* 71a)! And a jealous husband suspecting his wife of adultery had to have evidence of degrees that were often humanly impossible.

According to the twelfth-century Rabbi Moshe ibn Maimon (Maimonides), incestuous relations were forbidden because otherwise men would be inclined to take advantage of the women in their households, who were easily accessible and more prone to submit to the whims of the all-powerful male breadwinners upon whom they depended and under whom they were lorded. Anyone who thinks the twelfth-century rabbi was being too severe in his rationale ought to examine the data on incest in the *twentieth* century, which clearly demonstrates that a surprising number of female victims of sexual abuse are related to, or live in the same households as, their abusers. "All illicit sexual relations with females," wrote Maimonides, "share one thing in common, that in most instances these females are constantly in the presence of the male head of the house and thus easily accessible to him and also easily manipulated by him. Therefore, if the status of these females were no different from that of *any* unmarried female . . . most men would have given in constantly to their urges and engaged them in sexual relations" (*Moreh Nevuchim* 3:49). Psychotherapist Rachel Biale sums it up this way:

The purpose of the extensive incest prohibitions is perhaps to afford females double protection: by being included in the household they are protected from sexual advances and imposition from outsiders, since the males of the household are their patrons, and through the prohibitions on incest they are protected from insiders. (Rachel Biale in *Women and Jewish Law* [New York: Schocken Books, 1984], p. 181)

As Rabbi Luzatto points out, the restrictive laws about sex—whether divinely inspired or socially evolved—in no way were meant to downplay sexual activity or desire, but were meant, again, to keep the community as much as possible in a state of moral conduct and social orderliness:

The prohibitory laws regarding sexual intercourse were not intended to diminish sexuality, as is the thinking of Maimonides [*Moreh Nevuchim* 3:49]. After all, the Torah did not forbid marriage with many wives nor frequent sexual activity with one wife. Rather, these laws were instituted for the welfare of the society. For example, sex with another man's wife was prohibited in order to prevent the evils of coveting, conflict, and murder that could easily result from adulterous liaisons. And even if a man was *comfortable* with sharing his wife . . . this practice would only perpetuate an unhealthy situation that would in the end wreak havoc upon the nation as it would lead to the demoralization of the community. And the prohibition against sex between two men or between a person and an animal, is due to the fact that such acts are contrary to Nature, and if they were indeed permitted, the result would be a decrease in men taking women to wife and establishing families. . . . And two sisters married to the same man was forbidden to prevent the pain and jealousy that is more apt to occur between sisters than between two women unrelated to one another. . . . And it appears to me that the prohibition against marriage between brothers and sisters is for the benefit of the nationhood, for if sisters were permitted to brothers, most men would marry their sisters and consequently each family would almost become a nation of its own since there would not be breeding between families, and the nationhood would become severely divided into factions that would not be in harmony with one another but rather in conflict one with the other. (Luzatto in *Yesodei HaTorah* chap. 43)

Of course, if, as Rabbi Luzatto and other commentators posit, homosexuality was forbidden in order to keep nature's manufacturing plant in operation, then it becomes questionable whether there is anything specifically *Jewish* about this proscription, let alone *divine*, or whether it arose out of what *people* decided was productive and counterproductive to the perpetuation of their respective nationhoods, religions, and societies.

On the other hand, the very Bible that lists all these restrictions also recounts without inhibition the very open, liberal sexuality its key characters practiced. The narrative unashamedly tells us how Yehudah, leader of the tribes, heads down to the village in search of a prostitute (Gen. 38:15–16), how the patriarch Jacob embraces and kisses his cousin Rachel upon their initial encounter (Gen. 29:11), how the matriarchs Leah and Rachel negotiate with one another over who gets to sleep with the man they share as their husband (Gen. 30:15–16), and how the prophetess Ruth climbs into the bed of the man she hopes to marry (Book of Ruth 3:7). Of course, rabbinic commentaries have wrestled hard to discover alternate meanings and implications in all these narratives, including the biblical *Shir HaShirim*, "Song of Songs," which is by far the most erotic book of the Jewish scriptural canon. But the fact is that they read explicitly, openly, unabashedly, simply because they were composed long before the age of puritanism was ushered in, first by Graeco-Roman Hellenism and then by Christianity.

This lack of inhibition when discussing sexual desire and activity does not end with the Scriptures but continues as well in even greater detail in the Jerusalem and Babylonian Talmuds, the compilation of rabbinic law, lore, and exegetical interpretation of Scriptures that spans some 800 years, from around the third century B.C.E. through the fifth century C.E. While some talmudic narratives about sex acknowledge sexual lust but then downplay it, other narratives extol it and celebrate it as essential to human welfare and as a powerful gift from God that is to be harnessed not with shackles but with responsibility.

Primarily, the teachings around eroticism in the Talmud emphasize the immense power that sexual desire wields and how this overwhelming urge—especially in men—often distracts men from the more important tasks of living, both spiritually and physically. At the same time, the ancient teachers also remind us how this very same urge that so distracts us from the affairs of living is an extremely essential component of what exactly it is that makes the world go round. The mysterious force beind this "urge" is initially called *yetzer*, or "inclination," and later *yetzer hara,* or "evil inclination." Literally, the term *yetzer* means "something that is being formed"; it is the cauldron of creative churning and chaos that moves us toward positive or negative behavior and actualization. According to the ancient teachers, it was created in the sixth cycle of Creation, when the human was created. The rabbis point out how every cycle in the Creation story of Genesis ends with the verse "And the Source of Powers saw everything that had been made, and it was good," whereas for the sixth cycle of Creation the verse adds "and it was *very* good" (Gen. 1:31). Taught the third-century Rabbi Nachmon ben Shmuel: "What is the meaning of '*very* good'? This alludes to the creation of the *yetzer hara*, because without the *yetzer hara* no man would build a house or marry a woman or have children or earn a livelihood" (*B'reishis Rabbah* 9:7). The force within us that diverts us from the most important things in life is also the very force that enables us to *perform* the most important things in life. Like nuclear energy, the *yetzer* is in itself a neutral force that can be harnessed for either creation or destruction. We kill because of the *yetzer*; we also bring new life into the world because of the *yetzer*. Bottom line, the teachers of yore put it this way: "We serve God with *both* our inclinations, toward good and toward evil" (Babylonian Talmud, *Berachot* 54a); both can be channeled toward the sacred: the drive within us that inclines us toward that which is good, as well as the drive within us that potentially can incline us toward that which is bad. The sex drive in itself, in other words, is not evil, nor is it the primary domain of the *yetzer hara*. Every part of the human body, the rabbis taught, is endowed equally with both the possibility for evil as well as the possibility for good (*Zohar, Bamidbar* 234).

Unfortunately, many people assume that when Jewish tradition speaks of a *yetzer hara* and a *yetzer tov*, a good inclination and a bad inclination, that it is referring to two opposing forces within us, each vying for our attention, competing for our obeisance. But we are endowed only with a single *yetzer*, and whether it sways us to the good or to the bad depends on our deepest, most inner self and what choices emanate from that self. The same inclination that was personified in the man called Adolf Hitler just as easily could have molded him into a saint as into the devil that he ended up becoming. There is even a teaching in the Talmud that the descendants of Haman—who plotted the extermination of world Jewry in 357 B.C.E.—as well as the descendants of Titus—who destroyed the second temple and laid Jerusalem to waste—"taught Torah in Jerusalem and B'nai B'rak" (Babylonian Talmud, *Gitin* 57b and *Sanhedrin* 96b). Whether actual descendants of Haman and Titus later converted and became great Jewish scholars is not the point. The point is that the *yetzer* is capable of either the greatest ennoblement or the lowest depravity but that no one is intrinsically good or evil; rather, we are defined by the choices we make and the actions we commit or omit in any given moment. "Do not be so sure of yourself," taught the first-century B.C.E. Hillel the Elder, "until the day you die" (Babylonian Talmud, *Berachot* 29a).

The terminology of "good" and "bad" inclination is merely metaphoric, to help us to identify the positive and negative potentials of this mysterious force that drives us to either. The Talmud recounts how the sages once gathered with the intention of destroying the *yetzer hara* once and for all but then canceled the mission when they realized that, in so doing, they also would be destroying the very energy that stirs people to marry and have families and build homes and societies, etc. (Babylonian Talmud, *Yoma* 69b; *Shir HaShirim Rabbah* 7:13). By ridding humanity of the evil tendency of the *yetzer*, they realized, they inevitably would have to eradicate the good tendency as well because it isn't the force of *yetzer* that is problematic but the individual person behind the wheel of the *yetzer*.

Throughout the talmudic discussions about sexual desire, the ancient teachers remained liberal and open-minded up to a point. While sex and sexual lust are wholesome and sacred, they taught, excessive indulgence in this area easily could push a person over the line where the positive tendency of the *yetzer* force turns topsy-turvy and becomes negative. Approaching too close to this line, they taught, we enter a hazy, unclear, twilight zone of poor visibility and tricky illusion:

> Said Rava (fourth century): "The evil inclination first appears to you like a distant wayfarer. Then he becomes as a guest in your home. And before you realize it, he becomes your master." (Babylonian Talmud, *Sukkah* 52b)

There is nothing in the Torah, for example, that outrightly forbids Jewish men and women from embracing one another in greeting, yet ultra-Orthodox Jewish men and women will not even shake each other's hands, let alone embrace. To outsiders, this might appear ludicrous, extreme, overboard, but the program is not about sexual inhibition between the genders; rather, it is about staying out of the twilight zone, keeping one's distance from the gray areas, where it becomes difficult to determine the fine line between healthy and unhealthy sexual emotions and activity. It follows that the ultra-Orthodox Jewish community remains significantly low on the statistical charts of teen pregnancies, extramarital affairs, date rape, and so on. The lines remain clear because they are rarely approached close enough to blur their visibility. Halakhically, however—that is, according to actual Jewish law—there is no prohibition involving physical contact between the sexes. "The prohibition against physical closeness with those women who are forbidden to us even in marriage applies only when the intent of the closeness is to fulfill sexual desire and for the pleasure of sexual intimacy. And the main thrust of the prohibition is solely in that context. However, abstaining for anything short of this is solely a matter of piety, not law" (*Batei Kehunah*, vol. 2, no. 12 [p. 17]). Writes the eighteenth-century Rabbi Avraham Dovid of Butshatz:

> It is obvious that the prohibition against physical contact with those women who are forbidden to us even in marriage applies only to contact that is accompanied by sexual intimacy. This means that his intention at the moment of contact is to become intimate with her for the purpose of sexual intercourse, even if circumstances compel him to delay having sex with her until a later time during that same day. Which is not the case where he has no such intentions, then there is absolutely no cause to be concerned over him violating

any prohibition in the Torah. (*Ozer Mekudosh* on *Shulchan Aruch, Even HaEzer* 20:1)

According to the wording in both the codes of Maimonides and Rabbi Yosef Karo, any sexual contact short of intercourse between a man and those women forbidden to him—such as his mother, sister, another man's wife, or even his own wife during her menstrual period—is prohibited by rabbinic law but not by biblical law (*Mishnah Torah, Hilchot Isurei Bi'ah* 21:1 and *Shulchan Aruch, Even HaEzer* 20:1; see the responsa of *P'nai Yehoshua*, vol. 2, no. 44).

In most of the rabbinic discussions on the subject from talmudic times onward, it appears that the sexual urge is often considered synonymous with the *yetzer hara*, the evil inclination, and almost exclusively is this partnership designated to male sexuality. This is probably because rabbinic teachings up until this century have been primarily the domain of men. When men discuss sexuality, they can speak only for themselves and infer women's sexuality:

Said Rabbi Shim'on: "The sexual urge of men is far more intense that that of women." Asked Rabbi Yochanan: "What proof do you bring?" Replied Rabbi Shim'on: "Look into the marketplace and observe who is seeking the services of whom." (Babylonian Talmud, *Ketuvot* 64b)

The rabbis recognized, however, that as far as male sexuality is concerned, the urge is very powerful, often distracting, and required toning down so that a man could attend more fully to the sacred tasks of prayer, Torah study, and acts of lovingkindness. On the one hand, they taught, lust "removes a person from the world" (Babylonian Talmud, *Avot* 4:21), and on the other hand, they taught, "the world cannot exist without lust" (Babylonian Talmud, *Avot D'Rebbe Natan* [version 2] 4:2). Again, the Judaic teachings about sex have to do with paradox, not dualism. While dualism states that sexual desire is exclusively a physical phenomenon and is intrinsically evil, paradox states that it is both physical and spiritual and can manifest either as good or as evil. In fact, Judaism considers sexual desire and intercourse as very essential to the process of spiritual unfolding and evolving. As the thirteenth-century Rabbi Yitzchak mon de Acco put it: "Anyone who lacks sexual desire has as much a chance of evolving spiritually as a mule has of giving birth." Rabbi Yitzchak then tells the following story to illustrate his point:

> There was this man who upon passing the courtyard of a palace, heard the sweet song of the princess who lived there. Drawn by her voice, he peered through a breach in the wall and beheld the princess bathing. Overcome by the sight of her immense beauty, the man cried: "Oh, if only I could merit to be with her!" The princess heard his cry and shouted to him: "In the cemetery!" Not realizing that

her meaning was "not in this lifetime," the man rushed to the cemetery and waited for her. As she did not come, he spent hours there, then days, then months, fantasizing how it would be when she would arrive, and he invented all sorts of excuses for her delay, meanwhile embellishing his imagination with his anticipation and imaging her beauty and clinging tenaciously onto his lust for her. After many years, his deep yearning for her, having no physical form in which to become translated, transformed into spiritual yearning and blissfulness, and he became a very holy man who lived the remainder of his life in that very cemetery, and to whom people flocked from all over the countryside to receive from him blessings and healings. Thus you see how the physical attribute of sexual desire is essential for the achievement of spiritual bliss. (*Reishet Chochmah, Sha'ar HaAhavah,* p. 63)

Both ancient and medieval kabbalistic teachings reflect this paradoxical relationship between sex and spirituality, that the very selfsame urge that distracts you from matters of the spirit is the very selfsame urge that you need to pay attention to in order to *engage* matters of the spirit. Basically, it boils down to this: Whether sex brings you closer to your spirituality or diverts your attention *from* your spirituality depends on what kind of consciousness and intention you choose to invoke in the course of lusting and lovemaking. The great masters were not removed from their sexuality because of their saintliness. On the contrary, the more spiritually evolved you are, the rabbis taught, the more sexually evolved you are (Babylonian Talmud, *Sukah* 52a). Therefore, when they would notice a very attractive woman, the consciousness that they chose to invoke was one of appreciation for the mystery and aesthetic that we call beauty. Rather than ogling the woman and undressing her in their minds, they proclaimed: "Source of Blessing are You, *Yah* our God, Sovereign of the Universe, Who created beautiful beings in the world" (Babylonian Talmud, *Tosefta Berachot* 7:7).

The rabbis neither encouraged nor put down sexual preoccupation, but rather pushed for moderation, not as law or required religious practice, but as sagely advice for men oblivious to the incredible force that hovers between their legs. "There is a tiny organ upon the man," they taught. "If he hungers it, it becomes satisfied; if he satisfies it, it becomes hungry." This, the teachers claimed, was exactly what happened to the otherwise saintly King David that led him to have an affair with Bat Sheva, a woman married to one of his captains (2 Sam. 11:2–4).

Said David: "Master of the Universe! Your people call You the God of Abraham, the God of Isaac, and the God of Jacob. When will they call You the God of David?" Said God to him: "These I have tested. You I have not tested." Said David: "Then test me, I pray." Said God: "I will indeed test you. Moreover, I will even give you the advantage over the others by revealing to you the matter about which you shall be tested, and I will even reveal to you the time when you will be tested. I will test you regarding your sexual urge, and I will test you during this night." When David heard this, he said to himself: "I will ready myself for this test by subduing my sexual urge." All during that day he made love with all of his wives in order to subdue his sexual urge. "When the time of evening arrived, David rose from his bed and strolled along the roof of the royal palace and from the roof he beheld a woman bathing and she was very beautiful in appearance" (2 Sam. 11:2). And thus happened what happened. Therefore it is that there is a small organ upon the man. If he hungers it, it becomes satisfied; if he satisfies it, it becomes hungry. (Babylonian Talmud, *Sukah* 52b)

The power of the sexual urge and how holy men are not immune to it is an incredibly wonderful, recurring theme in the ancient Judaic writings, both in the Scriptures and in the Talmuds. Judaism does not build up its masters and heroes as above physical reality, as superhuman spiritual beings, but rather as down-home mortals subject to all the challenges and wrestlings and urges with which the rest of us are graced. The great rabbis of the talmudic period, often held by contemporary students as way above mortal needs and yearnings, are described throughout the Talmuds as grappling with their sexual urges, just like us lowly twenty-first century layfolk. The beauty of these narratives, both in the Jewish Bible and Talmuds, is that the tradition becomes therefore that much more accessible by coming across as that much more mortal. "The Torah," the ancient teachers remind us, "was not given to the ministering angels" (Babylonian Talmud, *Brachot* 25b), but to us real people, who are cast in real-life situations from moment to moment:

[The rabbis would often journey about the countryside collecting monies to redeem prisoners from Roman captivity.] Once, after redeeming several women from captivity they brought them to Nahardea to lodge at the home of Rabbi Amram the Pious (fourth century). After ushering the women up a huge ladder into his loft, Rabbi Amram asked them to remove the ladder as it took more than ten men to lift it. That night, while one of the women was walking about atop the loft, Rabbi Amram caught a glimpse of her in the skylight and was overtaken by her beauty. Singlehandedly, he lifted the huge ladder which required more than ten men to move, and he began to climb up to the loft. Halfway up the ladder, he stopped and cried loudly: "Amram's house is on fire!" The rabbis rushed into his house to extinguish the fire and upon not finding any they turned to Rabbi Amram, saying: "You caused us great terror for nothing!" Said he: "Far better is it that you were falsely alarmed concerning the house of Amram than you should be rightfully alarmed concerning Amram himself in the World to Come! [when all truth is revealed]" Then he drove the evil inclination from his person and it went out from him in a pillar of fire. Said he: "I see that you are fire and I am but flesh. Yet, I am mightier than you." (Babylonian Talmud, *Kidushin* 81a)

An incident happened with one of the disciples of Rabbi Akiva (second century) who sat at the head of twenty four thousand students. One day he went out into the avenue of prostitutes when he noticed one particular prostitute whom he found very attractive. He dispatched a messenger to her to negotiate arrangements for the evening. When evening came the prostitute went up on the roof of her abode and beheld him in the distance teaching at the head of twenty four thousand students with the countenance of a battalion commander and with the archangel Gabriel at his right hand. Instantly she said to herself: "Woe to me if I sleep with this man as a prostitute, for I shall surely forfeit a significant portion of the bliss that awaits me in the hereafter if I so do, and shall surely bring him to lose out as well. However, if I reject him I shall save him and myself from such consequence." When the disciple arrived that night to be with her, she said to him: "Why do you wish to cause yourself to lose all of what you've accrued in the World to Come on account of a single moment of pleasure in *this* world?" But his mind was not turned. Then she said to him: "My son, that place that you so love (the vagina) is more filthy and repulsive than any other place on the body. And there exists not a single creature that can withstand its scent." His mind was still not turned. Finally, she seized him by his nose and pulled his face down to her crotch. As soon as he smelled the scent of her vagina he was repelled and he never married his entire life. A Heavenly Voice was then heard, declaring: "This woman and this man are destined for greatness in the World to Come!" (*Midrash Eliyahu Zuta* end of chap. 22)

The story of Rabbi Akiva's incredible disciple reads like an X-rated fairy tale, but the point of the narratives is this: It is not out of the range of possibility for even so hoity-toity a holy man as Rabbi Amram the Pious—or the unnamed rabbi who had 24,000 disciples at his feet and the archangel Michael at his side—to (1) have intense sexual desire and (2) arrange to act on it. The purpose of the latter story is also perhaps to discourage oral sex or kissing in the genital area of the woman, which is described as "more filthy and repulsive than any other place on the body, and there exists not a single creature that can withstand its scent." Of course, it isn't the business of rabbinical authority to legislate what we do in the bedroom, nor is it our business to judge them for employing tales like this one. It is much simpler to speculate that the one particular sage who told this story back then projected his own tastes regarding a man kissing a woman's genitalia. However, Jewish law permits kissing "each and every organ on the body" during lovemaking (Maimonides in *Mishnah Torah, Hilchot Issurei Bi'ah* 21:9; *Rama* on *Shulchan Aruch, Even HaEzer* 25:2) and, contrary to the story, most men find the aroma of a woman's genitalia quite enticing.

There are a number of like stories in the Talmud that, while demonstrating how even saints lust, are balanced with a moral about how sexual overindulgence is good for neither the body nor the spirit:

It was said of Rabbi El'azar the son of Dordayo (second century) that there was not a prostitute anywhere with whom he had not already slept. One day he heard about a prostitute who lived far across many rivers and who demanded a purse full of *dinarim* from anyone who wished to lay with her. Rabbi El'azar took a purse full of *dinarim* [1 *dinar* = 100 pieces of silver] and journeyed across seven rivers until he arrived at her mansion. They were about to make love when she farted. Said she: "Just as this fart will never return to its place of origin, so shall the return (repentance) of Rabbi El'azar the son of Dordayo never be accepted." He went and wept between two mountains until his soul departed. A Heavenly Voice then proclaimed: "Rabbi El'azar the son of Dordayo has achieved his full station in the World to Come." (Babylonian Talmud, *Avodah Zarah* 17a)

Again, the power of the male sex drive is described with great exaggeration, sparing not even those who are very spiritually evolved, and then balanced with a moral about how all the energy, preparation, anticipation, and effort it can exact from a man could be deleted in a single instant by a simple turn-off like a fart. The theme once more is about the power of the *yetzer hara*, the evil tendency of the otherwise neutral force of *yetzer*, that it can shoehorn you into a spin of self-destruction through situations and feelings that are otherwise perfectly OK and wholesome. Sex is wonderful; wanting it so desperately that you withdraw your life savings and journey across seven rivers for it is not:

> For thus is the skill of the evil inclination, that first he tells you to do such and such good deed, and on the morrow he tells you to just do this and that innocent thing, until eventually he will have you worshiping alien gods. (Babylonian Talmud, *Shabbat* 105b)

The antidote to being driven by the *yetzer hara* across the continent for sexual gratification, the rabbis taught, is realigning your concentration from its obsession with sex to the bigger picture, to the rhythm of the cosmic heartbeat that pulsated long before you ever had so much as a notion of what sex was and that will continue pulsating long after your final orgasm. Sex, in other words, is an essential component of life, but life itself is much bigger than sex. The antidote, then, is Torah study or meditation because it draws you out of your tunnel vision, from what it is that you are preoccupied with or stuck with in the moment, and shifts your consciousness to the bigger picture. Torah, in other words, is the potion that shifts you from preoccupation with temporal means to a consciousness of eternal end-all. "Says the Holy Blessed One: 'I have created the *yetzer hara*, and I have also created Torah as its antidote'" (Babylonian Talmud, *Kidushin* 30b):

> If the *yetzer hara* confronts you, drag him to the House of Sacred Study, for there he is harmless. If he be hard as a rock, he shall shatter; if he be brazen as iron, he shall be broken in pieces. (Babylonian Talmud, *Kidushin* 30b)

When the wife of the Egyptian minister Potifar was seducing the patriarch Joseph (Gen. 39:7–10), it was the appearance of the image of his father, Jacob, that stopped him from giving in to his *yetzer hara* (Babylonian Talmud, *Sotah* 36b). Your *yetzer* moves you to desire; your *yetzer hara* moves you to desire what is not good for you or others. Your *yetzer* moves you to eat chocolate; your *yetzer hara* moves you to consume the entire box.

Yet the ancient rabbis were not as rigid about all this as most people would think. They advocated making peace with our lustful side rather than *slaughtering* it (Jerusalem Talmud, *Berachot* 9). If it got so bad you couldn't take it anymore, the teachings certainly urged you to go meditate or pray or roll in the snow, but neither did they rule out altogether the least preferred option of surrender. The only qualification for surrender, however, was to avoid making a fool of yourself or your community. If you cannot overcome the urge, in other words, don't drag everybody else into the muck with you; don't schlep everyone else with you on your seven-river trek. Go ahead and do what you gotta do, but shame on you:

> Said Rabbi Elai the Elder (first century): "If a man sees that his lustful inclination is getting the best of him, he should go to a place where no one knows him, cloak himself in anonymity, wrap himself in black, and do what his heart desires, and let him not profane the Holy Name in public." (Babylonian Talmud, *Kiddushin* 40a and *Mo'ed Katan* 17a)

It was hoped, of course, that by the time you went through the whole process of finding a black cloak in the closet and then made your way to some village where no one knew you, you'd maybe stir up a change of mind, perhaps become shifted by all this distracting activity so that you would lose the inclination altogether, stay home, and realize how silly you must look to yourself and to God, going through all this trouble and arranging all these props just so you could have a six-second orgasm. Wise, then, were the sages who knew better than to say "absolutely forbidden," which instantly would have sent you flying across those seven rivers in full regalia without a second thought about it. "The Torah speaks in a language addressed specifically to the *yetzer hara*," taught the ancient rabbis (Babylonian Talmud, *Kidushin* 21b), commenting on the Torah's instructions regarding the Jewish soldier who lusts after an enemy woman captive spotted in the heat of battle. Forbidding such a reckless, abusive action in the heat of combat would have worked for some but not for others. Even today, in an era of so-called sophisticated civilization and hoity-toity morality, we read of soldiers raping women in the heat of battle. The Torah, wise to the overwhelming force of the *yetzer hara*, particularly under duress, says to the soldier: "OK, we can't stop you from your urge to take this captive woman of your enemy, but first you must allow her a period of mourning over the loss of her family, then you must marry her and honor her fully as your wife. And if the marriage doesn't work out, you cannot sell her or return her to the POW camp; you must release her to her freedom" (Deut. 21:10–14). By the time the soldier was as little as a quarter into fulfilling even one of these prerequisites, he very well might have come to his senses and dismissed the idea altogether; or he might choose to go through with it, but in the end the captive woman becomes not a sex slave but a bonafide Jewish woman entitled to all the comforts, security, and conjugal rights reserved for all Jewish wives. Even if the soldier breaks down and has sex with the captive during the battle, he still becomes obligated to her and must take her home and marry her (Babylonian Talmud, *Kidushin* 21b). The lesson is clear: No one can stop you from giving in to your urges, but be prepared to take full responsibility for your actions and for their consequences, not only as they affect *you* but also as they affect others. The *yetzer hara* is a powerful force not to be taken lightly or dealt with recklessly. At the same time, it isn't necessary to get too obsessed with the subject to begin with, which, too, would be a compulsion one just as easily could attribute to the *yetzer hara*:

> It happened that Abbaye (fourth century) overheard a man saying to a woman: "Come, let us go away together." Thought he: "I will follow them so that I might prevent them from sinning." He followed them for three *parsa'ot* (equivalent of 8.4 miles) alongside a meadow. The couple then parted from one another, saying: "The walk has been a long one, and our companionship has been sweet." Then said Abbaye to himself: "If the *yetzer hara* had done this to *me,* I could not have withstood him." He then leaned against the door of his house and wept. An elder saw him grieving and said: "He who is greater than his fellow, his *yetzer hara* is also that much greater." (Babylonian Talmud, *Sukah* 52a)

Rabbi Abbaye's decision to spy on the couple to prevent them from "sinning" is reflective of how religion in general often goes too far with its "concern" about what we do in the privacy of our bedrooms. Yet the story is equally reflective of the depth of caring the ancient teachers demonstrated toward the spiritual, emotional, and moral welfare of their people. Rabbi Abbaye did not ambush the couple during the first tenth of a mile to warn them about the probability of intimacy resulting from their hanging out together for too long. Rather, he walked eight miles, giving the couple the benefit of the doubt that nothing unwholesome would necessarily unfold, yet prepared to intervene if it did. What a beautiful story of a master who cares so much for others that he takes hours out of his day just so that a romantically involved couple could have their rendezvous with responsibility and safety. He very well could have said: "Look, I don't have all day to kill, so I'll just go over to these teenagers right now and tell them to go their separate ways or find a chaperone." Obviously, the ancient masters had nothing against women and men hanging out with one another (e.g., Babylonian Talmud, *Baba Batra* 91b and *Mishnah, Ta'anit* 4:8). They weren't concerned with the force of attraction between the genders. In fact, they poked fun at holier-than-thou men who would go to ridiculous extremes to avoid their attraction to members of the opposite sex—thus the teachings about the *chosid shoteh,* or pious idiot: "What is a pious idiot? For example, a woman is drowning, and he says: 'It is not proper to look at her, so how can I rescue her?'" (Babylonian Talmud, *Sotah* 21b):

> There are seven types of pharisees. . . . the third kind is the pharisee who [is so cautious about not looking at women that he squints his eyes and] bumps into walls until his head bleeds. (Babylonian Talmud, *Sotah* 22b [Bracketed portion is *Rashi's* commentary])

Even some of the rabbis themselves were criticized for going too far in their zealous campaign against overpowering sexual urges:

> Rabbi Kahanah (third century) was a basket peddler. Once he came to the home of a certain Roman matron who bought some baskets from him and then began to seduce him. He excused himself, saying: "Let me first go and wash myself." He climbed up on the roof and jumped, but Elijah the Prophet came down from Heaven and caught him. Said Elijah: "You have put me through the trouble of journeying four hundred *parsa'ot* (equivalent of 1,080 miles)." Replied Rabbi Kahanah: "It is no fault of mine that my poverty forces me into such a risky business." Elijah gave him a potful of *dinarim* and returned to Heaven. (Babylonian Talmud, *Kidushin* 40a)

No reason to jump to your death for the sake of piety and thereby turn the whole divine scheme of things topsy-turvy. Just hang out with your sex drive, and keep your eyes on the road while you are driving or being driven. The *yetzer hara*, in other words, is not your enemy any more than is your car. It isn't anything external to who you are; rather, it is an integral part of your persona in the physical reality. It is the cauldron of utmost creativity, the source of your imagination, the power behind your will to be. Don't try to squelch your feelings and inclinations toward wholesome sexual experience for fear that those same feelings and inclinations just as easily can push you over the edge into unwholesome sexual experience (Maimonides, *Mishnah Torah Hilchot* De'ot 3:1). Eating too much is unhealthy, but you wouldn't think of cutting out eating altogether to prevent overeating. But if you try too hard to keep your sexuality suppressed so that you don't have to deal with it, be forewarned that you will end up dealing with it with far greater intensity than if you were to learn to get comfortable with it:

Rabbi Chiyya bar Ashi (end of third century) when he prostrated himself in prayer would plead: "May the Compassionate One save us from the *yetzer hara*." One day his wife overheard his prayer. Said she: "It has been several years since he has made love with me. Why is he praying for this?" One day he was studying in his garden when his wife clothed herself in enticing garb and approached him. Said he to her: "Who are you?" Said she: "I am Charuta the famous prostitute, and I have just returned today." He asked her if she would have sex with him. Said she: "Fetch me first some fruit from atop your pomegranate tree." He gave her the fruit and they made love. Afterward, she got back into her original clothes and began to warm up the oven to bake some bread when Rabbi Chiyya returned and climbed into the oven. She said to him: "What are you doing?" He told her what had happened [that he had made love with another woman behind her back]. Said she to him: "It was me!" He didn't be-

lieve her until she showed him the pomegranate he
had given her. Said he to her: "Nevertheless, I *intended* something that was wrong." (Babylonian
Talmud, *Kidushin* 81b)

Moderation is the prescription, not in frequency
of sexual activity or in creativity during lovemaking,
but in the parameters within which you play out your
lusting. Sex in a context that nourishes and bonds
both partners is radically different from sex in a
context where one or both partners only use one
another's bodies for their own pleasure, with no consideration of the mood or needs of the other. And
this holds just as true for married couples as it does
for single people. Marriage is not a license to masturbate on someone's body, which is what it becomes
when one or both partners have sex during unresolved marital difficulty that has resulted in resentment
or in pending divorce, or when one of the partners
is not in the mood (Babylonian Talmud, *Eruvin* 100b
and *Kallah*, no. 19; *Iggeret HaKodesh*, chap. 6;
Ba'alei HaNefesh, Sha'ar HaKedushah; *Shulchan
Aruch, Even HaEzer* 25:8). Sex must never be
forced; it must be consensual at all times and must
include a conscious honoring of the other *(Mishnah
Torah, Hilchot Ishut* 15:17). During this most intimate of all moments in a relationship, we are also
most vulnerable and most delicate. In fact, Jewish law
holds a man liable if he in any way injures his wife

during lovemaking (*Shulchan Aruch, Even HaEzer* 83:2). Taking an abusive husband to court was unheard of in ancient and medieval times, but in the Jewish community it was part of the theology. A man had as much license to hurt a member of his own family as he did some stranger in the street. Marriage was a license that allowed nothing but love and nurturance.

A woman's sexual space or time away from intimacy was guaranteed her not only by specifically designated periods such as during her menses, but at any time she felt she needed space from her husband: "A man should not hang around his wife all the time like a rooster," wrote the twelfth-century Rabbi Moshe Ibn Maimon (*Mishnah Torah, Hilchot De'ot* 5:4 and *Hilchot Isurei Bi'ah* 21:11; also in Babylonian Talmud, *Berachot* 22a). It isn't enough, the rabbis taught, for women and men to see each other merely as different genders. Rather, men and women ought to honor one another as completely different *nations* (Babylonian Talmud, *Shabbat* 62a).

The ancient rabbis did not presume to know the psyche of women, let alone their sexuality, and could only infer either from what their own wives taught them. But to play it safe, they instructed men to offer intimacy to their wives before setting out on a journey (Babylonian Talmud, *Yevamot* 62b), near the time of the onset of menstruation (Babylonian Talmud, *Pesachim* 72b), following menstruation (Jerusalem Talmud, *Ta'anit* 1:6), and at least once a week for scholars and mule drivers, twice a week for laborers, every day for those who are wealthy and don't need to work, once in sixty days for camel drivers, and once in six months for sailors (Babylonian Talmud, *Ketuvot* 61b). This schedule represented the *minimum* number of times a man was instructed to offer sexual intimacy to his wife—a precept the Torah calls *onah* (Exod. 21:11). The twelfth-century Rabbi Avraham Ibn Dovid (*Ravad*) reminds us, however, that the general rule of *onah* is "any time she so much as hints to him her desire for intimacy" (*Sefer Ba'alei Hanefesh, Sha'ar HaKedushah*). The sixteenth-century codifier Rabbi Yosef Karo also reiterates how important it is for a man to be attuned to the sexual needs of his wife: "such as if he sees her nursing their child and she hints to him her desire for intimacy and she is adorned toward that purpose, then is he obligated to satisfy her" (*Shulchan Aruch, Orach Chayim* 240:1).

The rabbis, then, strove to ensure that in the heat of male sexual passion, the woman would not be forgotten, neither in situations when she preferred *not* to have sex nor in situations when she *wanted* sex. In the former instance, the man needs to curb his sexual energy and avoid "pushing" on the woman's physical space; in the latter instance, the man should be sensitive to what it is the woman needs in order that she, too, might benefit from lovemaking, in emotional bonding and sexual gratification:

Both [Rabbi Avraham Ibn Dovid] and Karo emphasize the husband's obligation to be attuned and re-
sponsive to his wife's needs. They seem to have
similar views of female sexual needs as legitimate,
present throughout the life cycle, and in need of
protection. Both start with the same assumption,
that the laws of *onah* come to correct the natural
imbalance between men and women in sexual tem-
perament and power. (Rachel Biale in *Women and
Jewish Law* [New York: Schocken Books, 1984],
p. 133)

It is important to note here that men's sexuality
was taken into account as well and not merely left to
the assumption of chronic libido. On the contrary, a
man is not expected to have sex with his wife beyond
his ability and mood. Mood plays an essential role in
harmonious sexual relations, and it is no less wrong
for a man to *compel* himself to have sex with his
wife than it is to engage in lovemaking while feel-
ing *resentful* toward his wife, as discussed above
(Babylonian Talmud, *Eruvin* 100b and *Kallah*, no.
19; *Iggeret HaKodesh*, chap. 6; *Ba'akei HaNefesh*,
Sha'ar HaKedushah; *Shulchan Aruch*, *Even Ha-
Ezer* 25:8). Nor was the woman the only partner in
a relationship presumed to be in *need* of sexual intimacy. If a woman refused to have sex with her husband altogether, she was fined with the diminution
of the value of her *ketubah*, the ritual marriage contract that guaranteed a woman economic security in
the event of divorce, abandonment, or death. Like-

wise, if a man refused to have sex with his wife, he was fined with the *increase* in the value of her *ketuba* (Babylonian Talmud, *Ketuvot*).

Nevertheless, the ancient teachers also recognized that there are times when either a man or a woman simply might want a "break" from intimacy and that they ought not to be penalized by it. According to the first-century B.C.E. Hillel the Elder, a man had the right to abstain a maximum of one week, and according to his colleague Shammai the Elder, two weeks (Babylonian Talmud, *Ketuvot* 61b). Of course, the rabbis are discussing average situations, not extenuating circumstances such as a woman or a man who is healing from childhood sexual abuse or some other trauma that would make sex or physical intimacy in general a deeply painful experience, or such as a woman who declines to make love because her husband is repulsive to her in bed (Babylonian Talmud, *Ketuvot* 63b). Rather, they are talking about a normative marital situation, specifically *marital* because a nonmarital relationship carries no responsibilities or obligations between the couple other than what they have negotiated between each other, whereas a marital relationship carries certain responsibilities and obligations between the couple that are established by the very religious law that instituted the idea of marriage to begin with. Moreover, it is given that when two people get married, they expect physical intimacy and lovemaking to be an essential part of the program. The ancient rabbis further assumed that physical intimacy was so important to the woman in particular that if a man refused to make love in the nude and also demanded that his wife remain clothed during lovemaking, he must offer her a divorce and the value of the *ketubah* (Babylonian Talmud, *Ketuvot* 48a and *Yoma* 77a)—so much for the "hole-in-the-sheet" myth.

The sages of Israel were also sensitive to the fact that women through the ages—not solely in our contemporary era of feminist consciousness—suffered unceasingly from the unwanted glares and attention of men, forcing many cultures to so overdress their womenfolk that barely anything but their eyeballs remained visible. The rabbis' sensitivity to this rude, irresponsible behavior on the part of many men gave rise to the numerous teachings and rules about walking behind women or staring at women (Babylonian Talmud, *Berachot* 61a), even asking a woman to do something for you that you could do just as easily yourself (Babylonian Talmud, *Kidushin* 81b).

Many people assume that such teachings were and continue to be a put-down of women, and it is certainly possible that over the centuries such practices easily could have become misconstrued as such by mindsets bent on keeping women in a subjugated class by considering them temptresses and ritually unclean. But a closer look at the overall context in which these sorts of teachings initially appear offers us a picture not of a bunch of patriarchs aiming to keep women invisible and insignificant, but patriarchs aiming to keep women's dignity intact against an almost universal male attitude that considers women more as objects than subjects. The Talmud recounts, for example, how a man became so infatuated with the woman next door that he grew deathly ill. The physicians who examined him presented their prognosis to the rabbis and basically argued that if their patient did not have sex with this woman, he surely would die. When the rabbis forbade it, the doctors pleaded that the man at least be permitted to see her in the nude. This, too, was denied. Next, the physicians requested that the woman at least be allowed to speak to the man, even from behind a wall. This, too, was denied. "Better that he die," ruled the sages, "rather than the dignity of women be taken for granted, and lest such incidents increase as men would invent the ruse of illness in order to lay with women to whom they are attracted. Moreover, intimacy with her would not settle his mind anyway" (Babylonian Talmud, *Sanhedrin* 75a; see *Rashi*'s commentary).

It might seem unfair to "liberated" men of our enlightened new age that the ancient teachers seem to be picking on them, keeping them at bay like a bunch of salivating dogs, homing in on the hapless and innocent male gender, but the fact is that the male species continues to this day to be the primary perpetrator of sexual harassment and abuse both inside and outside the home and relationships. The ancient rabbis weren't interested in being politically correct, not for their time and certainly not for ours. Rather, they were interested in dealing with real-life facts and situations:

> There are three kinds of people whose praises are sung daily by the Holy Blessed One: the bachelor who lives without sin in a village, the poor man who returns a lost item to its owner rather than keep it for his own needs, and the wealthy man who gives to the poor anonymously. It happened that this teaching was being shared in the presence of the bachelor Rabbi Safra and his colleague Ravva. Rabbi Safra's face began to shine with pride when he heard this teaching. Said Ravva to him: "The teaching does not apply to bachelors like you but to bachelors like Rabbi Chanina and Rabbi Oshiya, who were shoemakers in Israel and lived on the street of the prostitutes, for whom they made shoes and to whom they delivered them. And while the prostitutes would inspect their handiwork, the rabbis would not raise their eyes to gaze upon them. And thus did people swear 'by the lives of the saintly rabbis of Israel'" (Babylonian Talmud, *Pesachim* 113b).

All these teachings convey the simple idea that women are not responsible for men's sexuality. Men are. And part of that responsibility involves curbing the *yetzer hara*, which means I should celebrate my sexuality and not squelch my lustfulness, but I need also to keep it in check so that it does not violate the boundaries of another. This is the balance for which the sages strove through the vehicle of all these teachings and stories: Sex is great, but it is also powerful. Therefore, enjoy it with responsibility.

2

HUMAN SEXUALITY
IN JEWISH LAW

PLEASURE VERSUS PROCREATION

It is a well-established fiction that Judaism allows sexual activity solely for the purpose of procreation. On the contrary, there is such a thing as physical love and pleasure in Judaism independent of procreative possibilities. If we merely penetrate and ejaculate to procreate, we humiliate. We are, after all, created in the Image of God, and that means we do not copulate like cattle in heat, which hump each other instinctively to propagate the species. It is ironic as well as tragic that the same teachers who tell us to become holy, elevated above all other creatures, also tell us to have sex like hippos. "Just as a lion tramples and devours and has no shame, so a boorish man strikes and copulates and has no shame" (Babylonian Talmud, *Pesachim* 49b).

There are of course those who will invoke the talmudic narrative of the third-century Imma Shalom, who described her saintly husband as making love to her, "as if a demon compelled him, and he would only uncover my body a handbreadth at a time and then cover it up again" (Babylonian Talmud, *Nedarim* 20b). But why must we read this story as implying prude behavior, rather than the complete opposite? Is it not just as feasible that her husband unleashed his passions and went wild with desire, "as if a demon compelled him"? As for uncovering his wife handbreadth by handbreadth, this could just as well describe a man who is revelling in every square inch of his lover's body, relishing every delicious moment of foreplay and lovemaking, rather than losing out on the fullness of the act. Imma Shalom's man paid attention to every part of her body, appreciating how she looked and how she felt. Someone who was in a hurry to get it over with would certainly not be wasting any time peeling the sheet or blanket from his lover's body one square inch at a time. Imma Shalom's pillow talk appears in the context of some rabbis complimenting her regarding her illustrious sons. Her response was that the way her kids turned out had a lot to do with the way in which they were conceived: through conscious, passionate, deliberate lovemaking. To interpret the story the other way around—that they were conceived through neurotic, unconscious, dissociated intercourse—is ludicrous.

Having sex for the purpose of having children is sweet and is a blessing—not a commandment (Gen. 1:28 and 9:1)—but it is not a contingency for having sexual relations, at least not in the Judaic teachings. Much of rabbinic leadership certainly has made it seem so over the centuries, but it is important to distinguish between Jewish law and Jewish survival. Jewish communities have suffered continuous persecution, expulsion, and decimation throughout history. It is understandable, then, that Jewish tradition would prioritize procreation to the point that it became an objective—if not a license—for sex. At the very least, Judaism deems sex as no less important for recreation than for procreation. In response to a yeshiva student who wished to know if it was OK to study books on sexual technique before he got married, the late Rabbi Moshe Feinstein wrote:

> The duty of a man to engage his wife sexually is not contingent upon whether or not there is the possibility of pregnancy, for it is mandated in the responsibilities of marriage that she should receive pleasure and not suffer, no different than the mandate that she be clothed and sheltered . . . (*Igrot Moshe, Even HaEzer*, vol. 1, no. 102).

In another responsum, this foremost rabbinic authority in the Orthodox Jewish community replied in the affirmative when a man asked if it was OK for him to marry a woman incapable of having children. The fact that the two people in question were very much in love with one another, it turned out, became a more important factor in Rabbi Feinstein's decision than the divine imperative to procreate: "Harmony between husband and wife is so precious that the Torah allows the erasure of the divine Name if it will preserve peace between husband and wife. I will therefore not be deterred [in my decision] by my respect for those great men [who ruled against a man marrying a woman incapable of bearing children unless he had already sired children with another]" (*Igrot Moshe, Even HaEzer*, vol. 1, no. 63).

Obviously, then, there is such a thing in traditional Judaism as sex for pleasure alone, for bonding. When the sixteenth-century Rabbi Yosef Karo ruled against bachelorhood, he posited that a man who already has brought children into the world and is living without a partner should remarry even a woman who is incapable of bearing children (*Shulchan Aruch, Even HaEzer* 1:8). In such an instance, too, there of course will be sexual activity, not for procreation, but for the sake of pleasure and for the relationship bonding that it provides. The eleventh-century Rabbi Yeshayahu de Trani ruled that extravaginal—i.e., non-procreative—ejaculation was permitted in the course of nice, healthy, sexual fun (*Tosefot Ri'd* on Babylonian Talmud, *Yevamot* 34b). In fact, in his discussion about the biblical prohibition against homosexual sex, Maimonides dismissed the notion that wasting of seed has anything to do with it (*Pirush HaRambam ahl HaMishnayot, Sanhedrin*, chap. 7). Which brings us to this question: If sex is not exclusively procreational but just as much recreational, what about homosexuality and lesbianism?

HOMOSEXUALITY

It will come as a surprise to many that the ancient teachers took time to grapple with the prohibition against male homosexuality and went so far as to limit biblically forbidden homosexual activity to anal intromission (Babylonian Talmud, *Sanhedrin* 54a– 56a, *Sotah* 26b, *Nidah* 13a; Maimonides' *Pirush HaRambam ahl HaMishnayot, Sanhedrin*, chap. 7). Some contemporary interpretations have gone further than the ancient teachers and *distinguished between homosexuality in the context of a loving relationship as opposed to the context of religious cultic regimen, the contexts in which the prohibitions seem to occur* (Lev. 18:3 and 22, 20:13 and 23; Deut. 23:18). The wording in the Torah, "A man may not lie with a man as with a woman" could perhaps imply a proscription against a *heterosexual* man having sex with another man, since a homosexual man would not be having sex with his lover "as with a woman." In other words, a heterosexual man should not *use* the body of another male to act out his desire to be sexual with a woman. Such grapplings are not unusual in Jewish tradition. Throughout Jewish history, the rabbis have wrestled repeatedly with scriptural writ when in certain periods and situations it blocked rather than furthered human physical and spiritual aliveness. "At times," taught the second-century Rabbi Shim'on ben Lakish, "the violation of Torah is its very preservation" (Babylonian Talmud, *Menachot* 99b). Even nonemergency issues such as divination and necromancy, which—like male homosexuality—are recorded as capital offenses (Lev. 20:27), managed nonetheless to get reinterpreted by the ancient teachers in such a way as to allow certain forms of occult activities (Babylonian Talmud, *Sanhedrin* 67b and 101a, *Eruvin* 43a, *Pesachim* 110a; *Bamidbar Rabbah* 11:5; *Kohelet Rabbah* 2:6; thirteenth-century Rabbi Menachem Meiri on Babylonian Talmud, *Sanhedrin* 67b; sixteenth-century Rabbi Yehudah Loew [*Maharal*] in *B'er Ha-Golah,* treatise 2, pp. 29–30). If ways were found to circumvent the capital biblical offense of invoking demons, for example, ways also can be found to reconcile the Torah's blanket prohibition against male homosexuality with those whose psychosexual orientations are inevitably at odds with that prohibition. The failure of the "mainstream" rabbinate to grapple with this issue today is more a result of homophobia than of halakhic or exegetical limitations.

LESBIANISM

Lesbianism, on the other hand, was never forbidden in the Torah to begin with, and while some rabbis in the talmudic period attempted to legislate against it, they were overruled. In the end, it was dismissed as merely "lewd," not prohibited, and punishable neither by biblical injunction nor rabbinic decree (Maimonides' *Pirush HaRambam ahl HaMishnayot, Sanhedrin*, chap. 7), and therefore inconsequential in Jewish religious and ritual law. The only attempted legislation regarding lesbian sexuality was by the third-century Rabbi Huna, who included lesbians in the category of those women who were forbidden to marry a *kohen gadol*, the high priest who functioned during the time of the Sacred Temple in ancient Israel. In the final ruling, however, Rabbi Huna's colleagues overruled him and merely passed a value judgment, not a *halakhic* injunction, calling lesbian behavior "immodest" (Babylonian Talmud, *Yevamot* 76a). But as the fourth-century Abbaya put it: "Since when did the Torah ever forbid immodesty?" (Babylonian Talmud, *Yevamot* 55b; *Sotah* 26b). Other rabbinic authorities tried to link lesbian sexuality to the Torah's prohibition against emulating the practices of the ancient Egyptians (Lev. 18:3), one of which allegedly was marriage between two women (*Sifra* on Lev. 18:3). However, even if there was indeed marital sanction of lesbian relationships in

ancient Egypt and Canaan, the practices forbidden
to the Israelites back then were strictly those associated with religious cultic rites alone, not social
customs (Babylonian Talmud, *Avodah Zarah* 11a;
thirteenth-century Rabbi Nissim of Gerona [*Ran*] on
Babylonian Talmud, *Avodah Zarah* 11a; sixteenth-
century Rabbi Moshe Isserles [*Rama*] on Rabbi Karo's
Shulchan Aruch, Yorah De'ah 178:1). Finally, we
do not derive halakhic ruling from homiletical or any
other form of exegetical speculation (Jerusalem Talmud, *Pe'ah* 9b; *Kohelet Rabbati* 6:2), which indeed
is why no prohibition against lesbianism was ever
legislated in Jewish law.

MASTURBATION

On the question of masturbation, which in Jewish law
is consequential only for men, it is erroneous to declare that Judaism has a blanket ban. Judaism rarely
has forbidden anything across the board, almost always qualifying its laws with a "but" or a "however,"
because Jewish law does not stand above or in spite
of the everyday, real-life human situation. If it does,
it is no longer *halakhah* but religious dogma, void of
aliveness and empty of meaning. It is, of course, sim-
plest for rabbinic authorities just to say no to everything rather than to wrestle with it. But like the
nineteenth-century Rabbi Shmuel of Salant once
said: "In order to be stringent you don't need to be

a scholar" (Y. Rimon and Z. Wasserman: *Shmuel B'doro* [Tel Aviv, 1961], p. 125).

Unfortunately, most of the stringent opinions codified in Jewish law reflect more the personal tastes of individual rabbis than what is or is not Torah standard. Proof of this is in the rabbinic commentaries that crowd the margins of the codes, often challenging the codifiers' rulings, or at the very least qualifying them. Let's examine, for example, the prohibition against masturbation as it appears in the codes of the sixteenth-century Rabbi Yosef Karo (*Shulchan Aruch, Even Ha'Ezer* 23:2, based on a discussion in the Babylonian Talmud, *Nidah* 13b, and Maimonides' codification in *Mishnah Torah, Hilchot Isurei Bi'ah* 21:18):

> It is forbidden to bring forth semen wastefully. And this sin is more severe than all the sins outlined in the Torah. . . . Those who masturbate by hand and bring forth semen—it is not enough for them that this is a prohibition of great magnitude, but one who does so is deserving of banishment, and upon them does the verse apply: "Your hands are filled with blood" (Isa. 1:15), and it is as if he has killed a person.

Comments the seventeenth-century Rabbi Shmuel ben Uri (*Beit Sh'muel*): "In spite of what is stated here and in the Zohar—that wasting semen is worse than all the sins of the Torah—it is not necessarily so." He bases his relatively lenient view on the twelfth-century Rabbi Yehuda the Pious's response to a man who asked him if he was allowed to masturbate: "[the man] feared that he would give into his temptation to have sex with a married woman or with a woman in her menstrual cycle. And [the rabbi] replied that it is better that he masturbate and waste his seed thereby than to, God-Forbid, succumb to the sin of illicit sex, but that he would also require some form of atonement afterward, such as sitting in ice if it was during the winter, or fasting for forty days if it was during the summer" (*Sefer Chasidim*, no. 176). The nineteenth-century Rabbi Shlomo Kluger was less rash about it: "[Masturbation] is permitted if it is to prevent one from sinning [by sex with a woman forbidden to him]" (his gloss on Rabbi Karo's *Shulchan Aruch, Even Ha'Ezer* 23:1).

Comments the eighteenth-century Rabbi Avraham Dovid of Buczacz (*Ezer M'Kodesh*):

> This is a matter about which there exists doubt whether the prohibition is biblical or rabbinical, and whether the verse the rabbis employ for it (Exod. 20:13, what is customarily translated as "You shall not commit adultery") is merely a supporting verse for their injunction or a specific biblical proscription against masturbation. . . . [According to the eleventh-century Rabbi Shlomo ben Yitzchak and others, it applies to adultery alone (*Rashi* on Exod. 20:13).] And since the source for this prohibition is doubly questionable (whether the verse in the Torah implies it, and whether it is a biblical prohibition or a rabbinical one) the principle is then that we incline to-

ward leniency, and we ought not to rule stringently about this doubly questionable issue. And even without all this discussion, it appears to me that the biblical verse used by the rabbis to prohibit it does not specifically imply masturbation but that the sages employed the verse to support their injunction against it. And at the very least it is possible that a one-time act of masturbation would then be permitted. Nonetheless, one should not permit this to begin with. . . . And though there are all sorts of disciplines of penance and confession prayers imposed upon one who masturbates, there is no cause or argument whatsoever for making all that noise about the sinfulness of it regarding someone who did it inadvertently. (on *Shulchan Aruch, Even Ha'Ezer* 23:2)

Commenting on the horrors that the kabbalistic Book of the Zohar attaches to the sin of masturbation and the intense regimen of penance it prescribes, the eighteenth-century Rabbi Yaakov of Emden writes: "One should certainly pay no mind to these gross exaggerations" (*Mitpachat S'farim* 1:20). Others share his opinion as well (e.g., *Tzitz Eliezer* 9:51 and *Av'nei HaEfod* on *Shulchan Aruch, Even HaEzer* 23). As the nineteenth-century Rabbi Menashe Grossberg put it in his responsum: "We rely on the *Rambam* (Maimonides) out of whose pure lips it has been said that the sin of masturbation is not an outright biblical prohibition" (*Shevet Menasheh*, no. 102).

The entire stringency in Jewish law concerning masturbation originates in the same talmudic discussion that also treats, with equal severity, the sin of holding one's penis while urinating, which the first-century Rabbi Eliezer likened to bringing a flood upon the world (Babylonian Talmud, *Nidah* 13a). If we want to reinforce the prohibition against masturbation, we ought then also to reinforce—or, more correctly, re-*introduce*—the prohibition against holding one's penis while urinating, against which the Talmud expended as much verbiage as it did with regard to masturbation.

As for the biblical Onan, he did not die because he masturbated. He died because he abused his brother's widow, Tamar. He was permitted to have sex with her only for the purpose of giving her a child, but instead he ejaculated onto the ground, thus frustrating her attempts to get pregnant (Gen. 38:8–10). Coitus interruptus, for example, is therefore permitted, according to many sources, if it occurs in the context of wholesome sexual relations (e.g., the thirteenth-century Rabbi Isaiah de Trani [*Tosefot Ri'd*] on Babylonian Talmud, *Yevamot* 34b), an entirely different context from that of Onan's sin. The term "onanism" is therefore erroneously used when applied without qualification to all circumstances of "wasting seed," such as masturbation or coitus interruptus.

The classical argument that extravaginal ejaculation of semen is tantamount to destroying life is challenged by such notables as the nineteenth-century Rabbi Menashe Grossberg, who considered such arguments unreasonable and in defiance of nature, reminding us that it takes the seed of both a man *and* a woman to form a child (*Shevet Menasheh*, no. 102).

Authorities such as the late Rabbi Moshe Feinstein also permitted "wasting seed" for purposes such as testing semen to determine fertility when a couple is having difficulty getting pregnant, though he suggested that such ejaculation take place not manually but in the course of lovemaking, either through the use of a condom or by masturbating against the woman's limbs (*Ig'rot Moshe, Even Ha'Ezer*, no. 70). Obviously, then, not all extravaginal or nonprocreative ejaculation is considered wasteful. In fact, the Talmud looks kindly upon nocturnal emissions, or wet dreams, which the rabbis considered healthy functioning of the human body and, in times of illness, "a good omen" (Babylonian Talmud, *Berachot* 57b). The sages of yore even went so far as to declare that "one who experiences an involuntary emission of semen on Yom Kippur may regard it as a sign from Heaven that all his sins are forgiven" (Babylonian Talmud, *Yoma* 88a [end]). And then there is the rabbis' acknowledgement that nocturnal emission is inevitable (Babylonian Talmud, *Yevamot* 76a).

It is apparent from all these sources that the Torah never forbade masturbation and that the ancient precodification rabbis only expressed their sentiments about it but did not legislate against it outright. It hurts no one and would only help adolescents, for instance, to cope better physically and emotionally with their overwhelming sexual inclinations. It is also likely to help them abstain from sex with a partner long enough to become adequately mature to do so in a context of wholesomeness, sanctity, and responsibility. We don't marry off our kids in their youth anymore, so we'd better find some alternative for them by the time they reach adolescence. Masturbation seems like a safe and viable alternative, and it is sad that United States Surgeon General Joycelyn Elders was fired in 1995 for suggesting it.

Bottom line, the principles concerning masturbation as discussed in the Talmud or as codified in the *Shulchan Aruch* are by no means the final word on the issue. *Halakhah* literally means "the walking" and has been a living process all along, never codified enough to become exempt from the challenge of situational reality. We live today in an age when promiscuity is rampant, especially among our youth, and to tell eros-ridden adolescents that they can neither engage in sex with one another nor masturbate is to push them to do both. We have to speak to our youth with the consideration of their burning compulsions and not build self-righteous walls against what is a healthy component of human spiritual and physical aliveness: sexual desire.

NUDITY

Another major misnomer about Judaism and sexuality is that of nudity. Almost everyone presumes that Judaism forbids nudity, or at least finds it disgusting and lewd. The following responsum on the question by the late Rabbi Moshe Feinstein will astonish a lot of readers, yet he is only voicing what always has been the traditional Jewish view on the subject—shocking to most of us, whose sexual values and mores have been fashioned more by Christianity's influence than Judaism's:

> [The idea of being dressed] out of respect to God—for His glory fills the whole earth—applies only during prayer, when one ought to be properly attired as one would in the presence of dignitaries. But if it is not during the time of prayer, then, although one is still in the presence of God, one does not need to be dressed in clothing at all, and it would be then sufficient to use any kind of wrapping to cover those parts of the body which are customarily covered, and this is because the whole issue of meticulousness around dress is based solely on social standards alone, which vary from place to place and from time to time. And so, barring the social factor, there are no particular requirements regarding the wearing of clothing. But the fact that we cover certain parts of our bodies irregardless of whether it is cold or hot, is evident that we consider those parts as shameful when they are

exposed, and for this reason it is shameful to stand around without a covering, not for social reasons [since it is in private] but out of respect to God. . . . But if sitting totally nude in one's house is not felt as shameful, then it should not be considered as such and one may sit thus in the privacy of one's house even without any covering at all upon those parts. . . . Therefore, the issue of *tzniyut* (modesty) that is taught by our sages concerning the proper conduct in the bathroom [to uncover only as little as needed to empty your bowels (Babylonian Talmud, *Berachot*, 63)] is only a matter of modesty for the individual, and perhaps it is to accustom the person to modest conduct in general. . . . These things are only pleasant customs and pious modes of conduct. . . . (*Igrot Moshe, Yorah De'ah*, vol. 3, no. 47:3)

In other words, if you are not comfortable about yourself in a particular disposition of dress or nudity, then that becomes sort of a barometer reading of what is respectful before God for *you*, which, of course, is subject to change if your feelings about it change. In yet another responsum on the subject, Rabbi Feinstein goes further out on the limb in his daring assertion that the question of nudity is not one of right and wrong or good and bad, but of personal tastes when you are in private and communal standards when you are in public:

> . . . The matter of *tzniyut*, that people go around entirely dressed, is not a result of any of the prohi-

bitions in the Torah. Rather, it is a careful and exalted practice to be attired even in private. . . . However, if it is uncomfortable because of the heat or for some other reason, then one may go about [unclothed] and there is not even a question of pious conduct in such an instance. . . . and God Knows of your discomfort. . . . And the standard [of *tzniyut*] is dependent upon what it is that makes one ashamed when standing before people, each place according to its custom. . . . And in a pressing situation, it is even permitted to pray [unclothed], for [nudity] does not interfere. . . . (*Igrot Moshe, Yorah De'ah*, vol. 3, no. 68:4)

Another very famous rabbinic "but" is the one about not making love with the light on or during the day (*Shulchan Aruch, Even HaEzer* 25:5). Again, further exploration of other rabbinic opinions on the folio of this ruling yields a whole different opinion. The seventeenth-century Rabbi Shmuel ben Uri (*Beit Shmuel*), for instance, distinguishes between engaging in sex directly in front of a light, as opposed to doing it somewhat veiled from the light source. Where Rabbi Karo forbids having intercourse "by the light of a candle even if the light is dimmed by the use of a blanket," *Beit Shmuel* quotes the ruling of the sixteenth-century Rabbi Yeshayahu Horowitz (*Sh'lah*), who permits it if there is a partition separating the couple from the light source. He then adds a few extra "howevers" of his own:

. . . Even if the room is lit up, it is permitted if the light is dimmed by a cloth. And if the light of the moon is shining through the window, it is permitted [to have sex in the moonlight]. So writes the *sh'lah*. However, further dimming of the light by a blanket over the couple is also necessary. And if a light is emanating from a second room it is permissible to have intercourse in that light, but it is possible that a blanket [over the couple] might be required also. . . . (on *Shulchan Aruch*, *Even HaEzer* 25:5)

At least in the case of a light shining in from another room, *Beit Shmuel* admits that it is "possible" that a covering might *not* be necessary because he implies that it is only "possible" that a covering *is* necessary. In black and white, then, we have it from the early rabbinic authorities that it is OK to have sex in a dim light.

Contrary to the standard assumption, the proscription against making love directly in front of a light is unrelated to the issue of whether it is permitted to gaze at one another in the nude. The light business has to do with the classic rabbinic emphasis on *tzniyut*, or modesty. Not that making love is immodest, but by *not* doing it directly in front of a light, we train ourselves in the ways of modesty, in a way of being in the world that is subtle, simple, quiet. The whole issue, as Rabbi Feinstein posits, is one of relative standards of modesty and sensitivity. And clearly the definitions of modesty vary from period to period and from society to society, as is reflected by the differing opinions about exactly how dark the room has to be during lovemaking.

LOOKING AT YOUR PARTNER IN THE NUDE

Gazing at your partner's body, however, is a whole other issue. The twelfth-century Rabbi Moshe ibn Maimon (Maimonides, or *Rambam*), for instance, ruled that a man is permitted to look at his wife even during her menstrual cycle, though she is forbidden to him sexually "even if he derives pleasure from it" (*Mishnah Torah, Hilchot Issurei Bi'ah* 21:4, and repeated in *Shulchan Aruch, Even HaEzer* 20:4). This means that a man certainly could gaze upon his wife during all other times, providing, of course, she is OK with this. Causing one's wife any form of discomfort or hurting her feelings is forbidden by other rulings elsewhere (Babylonian Talmud, *Baba Batra* 57a and *Baba Mezia* 59b). For those of us who would claim that Maimonides is referring solely to a clothed woman, his contemporary Rabbi Avraham ibn Daud (*Ravad*) adds in the margin of the text: "but he may not gaze at parts of her body that are ordinarily concealed," which clearly indicates that the case in question includes an undressed partner. On Rabbi Karo's rendition of the Maimonidean ruling, the *Beit Shmuel* adds to *Ravad*'s "but" and includes the genital area, which becomes standard (on *Shuchan Aruch, Even HaEzer* 21:4). In his commentary on Rabbi Karo's *Shulchan Aruch*, the eighteenth-century Rabbi Avraham Dovid of Butshatz (*Ozer Mekudosh*) writes: "the prohibition against a man looking at his wife applies only to her genitalia. However, gazing at any other area of her body is permitted—although one ought to guard oneself around this—and it is not included in the bounds of prohibition, for we must not add to the words of our sages" (on *Shulchan Aruch, Even HaEzer* 25:2). Rabbi Avraham Dovid thus offers us a broader picture of the rabbinic intent in telling us what we can and cannot do in the bedroom. It's OK to look, he says, but then adds that one ought to be moderate around this, and he finally admits that, bottom line, there is no prohibition against this whatsoever.

Clearly, the rabbis' concern about whether you're making love directly in front of a lamp or what part of your partner's body you're looking at has no basis in actual Jewish law; rather, it is more a part of the classic rabbinic objective toward ennobling and refining your behavior in general. Thus the rabbinic adage: "Sanctify yourself even in that which is permitted to you," which is often invoked following a permissive ruling about sex:

[Sexual intercourse] is permitted at all times, and anything they desire to do [with one another] is allowed, and every part of the body may be kissed, and [intercourse may take place] in any position, whether natural or unnatural, and by way of the limbs, so long as there is no wasting of seed. And there are some who rule leniently regarding this, and say that unnatural positions are permitted even if it *does* result in the wasting of seed [extravaginal ejaculation], as long as it occurs incidentally [in the course of lovemaking] and not with any regularity. Nevertheless, even though all of this is permissible, one who sanctifies oneself even in that which is permitted to them, shall be called Holy. (Sixteenth-century Rabbi Moshe Isserles [*Rama*] on *Shulchan Aruch, Even HaEzer* 25:2; based on Maimonides' *Mishnah Torah, Hilchot Issurei Bi'ah* 21:9)

The rabbis no doubt felt that the most opportune circumstance for planting the seeds of their idea of refined behavior was during sexual intimacy. After all, if you can retain a sense of sacredness even while you are letting your guard down and being your most uninhibited self, your chances of carrying that consciousness into everything else you do in life would be that much greater. Of course, the question is: Whose definition of sacredness—as with that of modesty—do we go by? And the answer is, as alluded to in the responsum of Rabbi Feinstein, that it varies according to personal tastes and sensitivity and according to individual societal mores, the latter determining standards of conduct and dress in public, and the former determining standards of conduct in the privacy of your own space.

VARIATIONS IN POSITION

Variations in position during coitus were left to the imagination of the consenting parties, even if the selected position would render impregnation impossible. While the third-century Rabbi Yochanan D'yahavai did attempt to legislate against any position other than "man on top," the majority of his colleagues overruled him, arguing that while the Torah regulates the kinds of food a Jew may eat, for example, it does not regulate the manner in which it is to be eaten, the amount of spices that may be used, or whether it is to be cooked rare, medium, or well-done (Babylonian Talmud, *Nedarim* 20b). Likewise, as the twelfth-century Rabbi Moshe ben Maimon (*Rambam*) codified, "whatever a person wishes to do during coitus is permitted, and they may engage in sexual activity whenever they desire and kiss each and every part of the body that they wish" (*Mishnah Torah, Hilchot Issurei Bi'ah*, 21:9).

Nonetheless, mainstream Jewish orthodoxy continued to propagate the overruled opinion of Rabbi Yochanan D'yahavai, and to this day most Jews assume that any position other than man on top is forbidden. Even the sixteenth-century Rabbi Yosef Karo's code of Jewish law, the *Shulchan Aruch*, fails to mention the talmudic ruling that all positions are OK, while mentioning the ruling of Rabbi Yochanan D'yahavai as if it were law. Out of the blue, a number of rabbinic authorities continually added the great "but" to all these liberal teachings about sex. Where Maimonides writes that everything goes and that sexual partners may "kiss each and every part of the body," later rabbis added: "but not her genitals" (e.g., *Beit Shumuel* on *Shulchan Aruch, Even HaEzer* 25:1, note 1).

Clearly, the Torah left the matter of sex up to our personal discretion, as clearly stated in the Talmud: "for while the Torah instructs you concerning what you are allowed to eat, it does not instruct you concerning how to prepare it, whether rare or well-done, cooked or boiled, spiced or unspiced, salted or unsalted . . . Rather, whatever [a couple] wishes to do [during coitus] is permissible" (Babylonian Talmud, *Nedarim* 20b). The Talmud then narrates how a woman once came to the second-century Rabbi Yehudah the Prince wondering whether it was really OK that she and her husband had made love in a position other than the man-on-top stance:

> Said she to him: "Master, I set the table for my husband, and he turned it over [i.e., I lay down on the bed to have sex with him on top, and he rolled over so that I was on top of *him*; or—he turned me over and entered me from behind]," Said Rabbi Yehudah to her: "My daughter, the Torah permits you; it is out of my hands." (Babylonian Talmud, *Nedarim* 20b)

It is noteworthy that the standard interpretation of this story has the woman presenting her question as a complaint against her husband and that Rabbi Yehudah's response was basically: "What can I do when the Torah allows your husband to do whatever he wants with you?" This is a shocking interpretation when set against the backdrop of all the scriptural and talmudic teachings forbidding a man from forcing a woman in sex, whether he is married to her or not. On the contrary, according to both ancient and medieval rabbinic teachings about sex, the emphasis is consistently on the husband's responsibility to *please* his wife and her sexual pleasure's precedence over his own. But all of that notwithstanding, the wording of Rabbi Yehudah's response contradicts such a shocking interpretation outright. He doesn't tell her: "My daughter, the Torah permits *him*," but rather: "My daughter, the Torah permits *you*," a clear indication that she wasn't complaining about her husband's "abnormal" desires, but, rather, was asking whether it was OK for *her* to be a willing participant in sexual positions other than what she had presumed to be the only kosher one.

Although "abnormal" positions during intercourse might result in "wasting seed," it was permitted nevertheless because the extravaginal ejaculation occurred inadvertently in the course of the act (sixteenth-century Rabbi Moshe Isserles [*Rama*] in *Shulchan Aruch, Even HaEzer* 25:2). According to the eleventh-century Rabbi Yeshayahu de Trani, even premeditated coitus interruptus is allowed in instances when impregnation poses a threat to the woman's physical or emotional health, or if the intention is for pleasure alone (*Tosefot Ri'd* on Babylonian Talmud, *Yevamot* 34b). The biblical sin of "onanism," it was argued, did not apply in such instances because the intentions were altogether different. Onan, the son of the patriarch Judah, died because he abused his sole purpose in being permitted to make love with his brother's widow, Tamar: to give her children. Instead, he used Tamar for his own pleasure and gave her nothing. This was the sin—not the spilling of seed in general, but the deliberate spilling of the very seed that was the only reason for him to have sex with her (Gen. 38:9; Babylonian Talmud, *Yevamot* 34b).

Onanism, then, is not about wasting seed. It is about abusing women.

FEMALE SEXUALITY

Female sexuality was perceived in a totally opposite manner in the Judaic tradition than in the teachings of the self-proclaimed "daughter religions." In the former, sex was the privilege of both parties; in the latter it was the man's privilege and the woman's duty. In Judaism, it is also the man's *responsibility* to satisfy his wife sexually. Although the notion of female orgasm did not bless the annals of Western medical literature until the nineteenth century, it long had been part and parcel of Jewish theology and law: ". . . and her food, clothing and sexual needs shall you not diminish" (Exod. 21:10). The thirteenth-century Rabbi Moshe ben Nachmon (*Ramban*) interpreted the Hebrew for this verse to read: "You shall not deprive her of physical closeness, appropriate bedding, and sexual gratification" (*Ramban ahl ha-Torah* on Exod. 21:11, based on a discussion in the Babylonian Talmud, *Ketuvot* 47b–48a). The ancient rabbis deemed a woman's sexual needs so important that they permitted a bride to forego her legal rights to everything in the marriage contract but sexual gratification. The deprivation of her sexual needs, it was ruled, would constitute a "physical hardship," whereas the other marital rights, from which she had the right to exempt her husband, concern themselves only with external goods (Babylonian Talmud, *Yevamot* 118b).

The Talmud even took the startling position that women possessed a far greater sexual capacity than men (Babylonian Talmud, *Baba Metzia* 84a); indeed, women do have the capacity for multiple orgasms, while men generally do not. On the other hand, men might be more *desperate* than women in their need for sexual release due to the buildup of sperm surplus and due to the external situation of their genitals and their resultant vulnerability to frequent stimulation. The ancient teachers therefore encouraged —almost mandated—foreplay, the absence of which during intercourse was considered lewd and beastly, a boorish act of irresponsible oblivion to the female partner's more complex sexual needs and capacity

(Babylonian Talmud, *Eruvin* 100b). The rabbis realized that the male's sexual drive focused primarily on the urgency of ejaculatory release, whereas the woman's sexuality constituted very intense emotional considerations as well as physical responses in areas of her body other than the genitalia. Bouquets of praise therefore were heaped upon the man who maintained ejaculatory control long enough for his female partner to climax first, assuring thereby that, in the heat of his own urgency, he would not neglect his partner's needs (twelfth-century Rabbi Avraham ibn Daud [*Ravad*] in *Sefer Baalei HaNefesh*, p. 139 of Masorah edition, Jerusalem). As Rabbi Moshe ibn Nachmon wrote to his son:

> Engage her first with words that put her mind and heart at ease and bring her joyfulness. Thereby will your thoughts and your intentions be in harmony with hers. Speak to her words which arouse her to passion, to union, to love, to desire, to eros. . . . and hurry not to arouse your own passion unitl her mood has become aligned with yours. Then, begin in love, and let her orgasm first. . . . (*Iggeret HaKodesh*, p. 189 in the Jerusalem edition)

SEXUAL COMPATIBILITY

Sexual compatibility, it follows, was also of utmost importance in the eyes of the rabbis of yore. After all, what good is there in all this talk about having a good time in the bedroom when there was no chemistry? In fact, if a woman found her husband repulsive in bed, she maintained the right not to have sex with him (Babylonian Talmud, *Ketuvot* 63b) and also had sufficient grounds for divorce plus settlement (Maimonides in *Mishnah Torah*, *Hilchot Ishut* 14:8). Rabbi Yehudah the Pious even went so far as to attribute the source of this principle to the biblical verse "A man who finds a woman to be with, finds goodness and obtains favor from God" (Prov. 18:22). "All sexual matters," wrote the twelfth-century mystic, "must take both his and her wishes into consideration. If a man finds a woman whose wishes coincide with his in these matters, then he has 'obtained favor from God'" (*Sefer Chasidim,* no. 509).

CONDITIONS FOR SEX

The rabbis realized, however, that there was more to an optimally satisfying sexual relationship than compatibility and performance. Diet, too, was an important consideration, as was time of day, place, and mood. The most respected codes of Jewish law—those of the twelfth-century Rabbi Moshe ben Maimon and the sixteenth-century Rabbi Yossef Karo—suggest strongly that the sex act take place not in the early part of the evening or during the day, but rather very late into the night, when there would be the least chance of distracting noises from the street or the household. Lovemaking also was discouraged immediately following a heavy meal, when the circulatory system would be preoccupied with the digestive processes, or during a time when either partner was hungry. Sex while intoxicated also was frowned upon because (1) there would be little or no conscious appreciation of the act, or conscious expressions of love, and (2) chances were likely that the male partner would become impotent, setting into motion a chain reaction of inadequacy complexes all too familiar to men who at one time or another have failed to "perform." Sex also is disallowed if you're thinking of divorce, if you hate your partner, or if you and your partner have just had a serious argument that has left you both upset with one another. Making love to one partner while fantasizing about another is also a no-no. Finally, and most importantly, it is forbidden for a man to engage his wife in sex against her will. Marriage, Judaism teaches, does not constitute license to rape (Babylonian Talmud, *Eruvin* 100b; Maimonides' *Mishnah Torah, Hilchot Issurei Bi'ah* 21:12; Rabbi Karo's *Shulchan Aruch, Even HaEzer* 25:2–10). All these laws add up to one basic principle: No human being has any right to *use* another human being.

In conclusion, it is apparent that Judaism traditionally does not regard sex as taboo; rather, sex is viewed as a positive, wholesome, sacred means to further both human relationships and spiritual self-development. To suppress its expression unnecessarily is tantamount to declaring that we know ourselves better than does our Creator:

> Taught Rabbi Zechariah: "In the Future, everyone will have to give an accounting before the Creator for all that their eyes had beheld and they did not partake of it." (Jerusalem Talmud, *Kidushin,* end of chap. 4)

NONMARITAL SEX

To this day, if you were to ask a Jew whether Judaism allowed sex without marriage, the answer would be "of course not." For many single Jewish women and men, this misconception about their own tradition has alienated them from their religion. How could you be a good Jew if you lived in sin? And many single people have found it difficult to entertain the idea of celibacy until marriage. It isn't like the old days, when people got married in their early teens.

On the contrary, however, from biblical times on, Judaism never decreed that you had to marry in order to have sex. Throughout the Jewish Scriptures, we read about the consensual, nonmarital relationship called *pilagshut*, or, literally, "half marriage." The woman in such a relationship was called *pilegesh*, or "half wife," not as it is customarily and derogatorily translated: "concubine." This form of relationship was prevalent even among the holiest of people, such as Abraham, Hagar, Jacob, Bilhah, Zilpah, Gideon, Caleb, David, Solomon, ad infinitum!

The *pilagshut* relationship was a sanctioned alternative to marriage, and no one back then gave it a second thought. Two consenting adults of the opposite sex simply decided to live together, and that was that. They even had children within such non-marital relationships, and nobody said "boo"; there was no stigma of illegitimacy—strictly kosher. The only requirement was the couple's observance of the menstrual laws.

NIDAH: THE MENSTRUAL LAW

The biblical laws regarding sex and menstruation forbade a woman and a man from having sexual intercourse while she was menstruating (Lev. 18:19 and 20:18). The couple was permitted to resume sexual relations only after seven days had passed since the onset of her period and only after she subsequently had immersed herself completely in a natural gathering of year-round waters, such as a lake, ocean, nonseasonal river, or *mikveh*, a ritual pool deliberately constructed by the community for this purpose.

During the second century, Rabbi Yehudah the Prince decreed for those women unlearned in the laws of *nidah* that they ought to count seven "clean" days from the time their period ended (Babylonian

Talmud, *Nidah* 66a). Thus, if a woman's period
lasted two days, for example, she now had to count
seven extra days so that her time of abstention from
her man now extended from seven to nine days.
What happened, in essence, is that the biblical laws
about nonmenstrual bleeding, i.e., *zavah*, or diseased
bleeding (Lev. 15:25)—which applied to both women
and men—supplanted those about menstrual bleeding (Lev. 15:19). Menstrual bleeding meant seven
days of sexual abstention, and nonmenstrual uterine
bleeding meant the number of days of the actual
bleeding plus seven days of making sure it was over,
which made sense for preventing the spread of disease. It is alleged that the women of the Second
Century were not learned enough in the laws of *nidah*
to determine which flow was which, so an across-the-
board decree established that every flow required the
seven clean days count, as is mandated for a *zavah*,
or diseased flow. Yet the eleventh-century Rabbi
Shlomo ben Yitzchak [*Rashi*] made it clear that if no
staining occurred for three consecutive days within
at least an eleven-day time preceding the onset of
menstruation, there is no fear of the woman being a
zavah gedolah, or with diseased flow, which would
have required the seven clean days count (on Babylonian Talmud, *Nidah* 66a).

In the fourth century, the original biblical seven-
day period of abstention was extended further to a
minimum of twelve days: a minimum of five days for
menstruating, followed by seven days of vaginal ex-

aminations to make certain the staining had ceased completely. The fourth-century Rabbi Zeyra alleges these extra days to have been the invention of the women (Babylonian Talmud, *Nidah* 66a). Yet the all-male rabbinic institution seems to have gotten quite involved in developing intricate laws and what-ifs relating to these seven "clean days." It is believed that the five-day minimum resulted from the fear that if a woman had sexual relations just before the onset of her period and her menstrual bleeding lasted only three days, she might discharge semen from the love-making three days ago along with some residual menstrual blood, thereby nullifying the seven clean days count she might have begun on day four. By waiting five days before counting the seven, this would be avoided. Interestingly, some of the greatest halakhic authorities ruled that this three-day wait due to seminal discharge was unnecessary if the woman simply washed her vagina with warm water (e.g., thirteenth-century Rabbi Mordechai in *Hilchot Nidah*, end of Babylonian Talmud, tractate of *Shavuot*). Others held that the three-day wait before counting the seven clean days was now unnecessary because the seminal discharge would upset the seven-day count only in regards to the Sacred Temple rites in ancient times, not in regards to marital relations (twelfth-century Rabbi Avraham ibn Daud [*Ravad*], quoted in *Nodah B'Yehudah, Yorah De'ah*, no. 127). The thirteenth-century Rabbi Moshe ben Nachmnon went further than most of the others and ruled that seminal discharge ought not to be a concern here because the menstrual flow certainly flushed out all the semen. And according to the eleventh-century Rabbeinu Tam, the concern is only if the woman had intercourse with a man who had ghonnoreal discharges (fourteenth-century Rabbeinu Asher [*Rosh*] on Babylonian Talmud, *Nidah* 66a, or no. 4:1). "One who is lenient about this has precedence upon which to rely regarding this stringency, for it is only a custom" (*Imrei Yosher*, vol. 2, no. 92). In the early part of the twentieth century, the kabbalist Rabbi Avraham Yitzchak Cook reiterated in his responsa that this whole seven-day count business is a custom the women of the fourth century took on and does not bear the weight of rabbinic decree because only a single rabbi, Rabbi Zeyra, sanctioned it (*Da'at Kohen*, no. 84). These discussions only mention Rabbi Zeyra's statement and hardly refer to Rabbi Yehudah's original seven-day decree because the latter's teaching applied to specific communities where the people were unlearned in the laws of *nidah*, whereas the former's teaching announced a general custom that the women voluntarily took upon themselves and that became binding to this day. Yet Rabbi Cook, for instance, reminds us that it takes a rabbinic court of seventy-one to enact a decree and the custom of the women in Rabbi Zeyra's time was never turned into an ordinance as such.

During the period between the second and fourth centuries two separate incidents are recorded of the adoption of stringent practices around *nidah*, one more strict than the previous, and both indicating that women were becoming less and less learned in the ritual laws around *nidah*. It may seem astonishing that there would be so drastic a drop in women's knowledge, especially when it concerns women's bodies and biological cycles. However, in examining the oppressive circumstances during the history of that era, we discover that the Jewish people in general were losing their connectedness with the earth and consequently with their bodies. This was an age during which this once earthy people was being deprived of their heritage of living on the land and of being attuned to Nature, both theologically and cosmologically. Gradually, as the Roman Empire became the *Holy* Roman Empire, the Jews (not unlike other indigenous peoples subjected to the agenda of Greco-Roman Hellenism and subsequently the Church), were increasingly severed from their earth-consciousness in spirit and in body. Therefore, it was not for any sudden lack of learning that the daughters of Israel adopted these precautionary measures but most probably because of an ebbing confidence in their abilities to always determine exactly what was happening in their bodies—whether their cyclic flow was menstrual or not.

It was up to the woman to declare both the onset and conclusion of her period (Babylonian Talmud, *Nidah* 11b, 12a, 16b) and immerse herself in a natural gathering of living waters prior to resuming, or commencing for the first time, sexual activity with a man. According to the ruling in the Talmud, the teachings of the ancient rabbis some 1,600 to 2,200 years ago, the biblical prohibition of sex with a woman during her period applied only to actual intercourse, not to anything short of that (*Pirush HaRamban ahl Sefer HaMitzvot L'HaRambam*). Heavy petting between a man and a menstruating woman was considered lewd, taught the fourth-century Rabbi Padas, "and since when did the Torah forbid lewdness?" (Babylonian Talmud, *Yevamot*, 54b and 55b).

The laws of *nidah* were originally part of the laws surrounding the Sacred Temple rites in ancient times. In fact, *nidah* is the sole remnant of those laws practiced even after the destruction of the Temple. According to these laws, then, once a single woman had ritually immersed herself in a natural gathering of living waters, she would be permitted to engage in lovemaking with a man.

Adultery and the Double Standard

Neither a single man nor a married man could have sex with a married woman, but a single woman could have sex with either a single man or a married man, and a married woman could have sex only with her husband. Nonetheless, in order for her to commit the cardinal transgression of adultery, Jewish law required that there was actual intercourse, not just heavy necking and "making out" (*Pirush HaRambam ahl HaMishnayot, Sanhedrin*, chap. 7). A married man, on the other hand, was permitted to have sex with a single woman or to marry other wives in addition to his original wife, provided he could support and sexually gratify each one accordingly (Babylonian Talmud, *Yevamot* 65; *Mishnah Torah, Hilchot Ishut* 14:3; *Ramban ahl ha-Torah* on Exod. 21:11). Nevertheless, a woman maintains the right to stipulate in her marriage contract, or *ketubah*, that her husband may *not* take on any additional wives (*Igrot Moshe, Even HaEzer,* vol. 3, no. 28, paragraph 7).

The double standard here possibly is based more on patriarchal possessiveness than on actual divine will and perhaps grew out of the need to identify progeny. You never can be as sure about who the father is as you can about who the mother is. One woman sharing several men indeed would leave the child's maternal identity clear but obscure the fraternal identity. In a patriarchal society, this would leave the men childless. On the other hand, if one man has many wives, we are sure not only of who the mothers are but also of who the father is. Lakme Batya Elior, a contemporary Jewish feminist writer and teacher, posits a second possible intention behind the institution of marriage:

Marriage was invented as a way of forcing a patriarchal society to provide women with economic security. In return, the woman agrees to absolutely guarantee that any child born after the ceremony will be the genetic descendant of her husband. And the laws regarding adultery—that is, a man sleeping with a woman who is married or ritually engaged to another man—serves as an enforcement of the woman's guarantee to her husband of progeny. So, the woman in a marital situation promises that she will not have sex with anyone else and is in turn promised that her husband and/or his family will support her and her child at the same level of lifestyle the family enjoys, during her marriage as well as in the event of divorce or if she becomes widowed. A woman in a nonmarital situation has none of these promises whatsoever. . . . but she does have the advantage of enjoying the same sexual and relationship mobility as a man, and her children are entitled to any paternal inheritance. (*Pilegesh Relationships: A Responsa* by Lakme Batya Elior, published in *Pumbedissa Journal* [vol. 2, no. 3], p. 11)

PILAGSHUT: THE NONMARITAL SEXUAL RELATIONSHIP

Indeed, the loophole in the classic adultery double standard was the *pilegesh*, the single woman who chose to be with a man without marrying him. If she chose to engage a second man, it wouldn't be considered adultery because she did not subject herself to the institution of marriage, which would have committed her fidelity to her husband alone. However, if a *pilegesh* wished that the estate of her lover support her child, she needed to remain faithful to him at least long enough to establish that the child was actually his. Once that was established, the child became eligible for the father's support and inheritance, like any other child. Thereafter, the woman could leave for another man if she so chose, without the hassle of divorce proceedings. "As she goes in, so she goes out" (Babylonian Talmud, *Gitin* 71a; Jerusalem Talmud, *Kidushin* 1:1).

The only hesitancy about *pilagshut* on the part of some medieval rabbinic authorities was the fear that a single woman in a living-together relationship might be too embarrassed to immerse herself in the *mikveh*, or the ritual pool, following her menstrual cycle (*Shulchan Aruch, Even Ha-Ezer* 26:1). The embarrassment referred to here is not due to any wrongness, but to the taboo that would have resulted from *pilagshut* having been discontinued for so many centuries. Customarily, the women who immersed themselves in the communal *mikveh* were married women closing their menstrual periods so that they could resume physical intimacy with their husbands. The only exceptions have been women undergoing conversion and a bride on the day before her wedding, in order that she could become physically intimate with the groom.

However, other rabbis, such as the eighteenth-century luminary Yaakov of Emden, dismissed rabbinic fears that a single woman might forego ritual immersion because of embarrassment and certainly did not feel that such possibilities constituted legitimate cause for legislating against nonmarital sex. Rather, a single woman living with a man, he wrote, "ought to feel no more ashamed of immersing herself in a communal *mikveh* at the proper times than her married sisters" (*Sheylot Ya'avetz*, vol. 2, no. 15).

Rabbi Yaakov of Emden then goes on to stress the equal legitimacy that a living-together relationship shares with the institution of marriage:

> Those who prefer the *pilagshut* arrangement may certainly do so. . . . For perhaps the woman wishes to be able to leave immediately without any divorce proceedings in the event she is mistreated, or perhaps either party is unprepared for the burdensome responsibilities of marital obligations, etc.; in such cases, for example, the Torah offered the option of *pilagshut*, a relationship that is mutually initiated orally and terminated orally . . . Marriage is not mandatory. . . . And those who claim that *pilagshut* is a violation of a biblical injunction to marry, are mistaken. . . . for the Torah did not mandate marriage, only that the human "be fruitful and multiply" (Gen. 1:28 and 9:1) . . . and this can be accomplished properly in a nonmarital relationship as well. . . .

Rabbi Yaakov's seemingly radical views lose their novelty as one further explores the writings of lead-ing rabbinic authorities who walked the planet long before his time. In the thirteenth century, for example, Rabbi Moshe ben Nakhmon (*Ramban*) was asked whether an out-of-wedlock sexual relationship was permitted. His response was:

> I do not know why there is any cause for doubt in the first place, for of course is this woman permitted to this man [without marriage] since she lives with him, and nonmarital sex was prohibited to Israel only by the teaching of Rabbi Eliezer ben Yaakov (third century) who taught: "One should not live with a woman in this land and with another woman in a second land, lest their offspring unknowingly marry one another, and brother will then marry sister" (Babylonian Talmud, *Yoma* 18b). However, if she comes into his house and lives with him and is known to him . . . she is permitted to be with him sexually. . . . and we have not found in either the Scriptures or the Talmud that there is any difference between a king or a commoner in this regard, and we find that the foremost spiritual leaders of Israel lived so. . . . And lest you claim that the Scriptures permitted this but that the rabbis later prohibited it, pray tell, then, in what place is it written that such a decree was ever pronounced? And which rabbinic court proclaimed it? And in what period of our history? (*T'shuvot HaRamban*, no. 2 [or *T'shuvot HaRashba*, no. 284])

So, while there are numerous rabbinic sources that forbid nonmarital sexual relationships outright, there are just as many, if not more, that permit them (e.g., *Kol Bo*, end of *Hilchot Ishut*; *Ritva* in *Birkei Yosef*, no. 101; *Mishpatim Yesharim*, vol. 2, no. 170; *Ravad* on *Mishnah Torah, Hilchot Ishut* 1:4; *T'shuvot HaRan*, no. 68; *Sefer haMitzvot haKatan*, no. 186; *Taalumot Lev*, vol. 3, 32:1, etc.). Moreover, the offspring of such unions, it was ruled, even had inheritance rights (*T'zeidah L'derech*, vol. 3, 1:2) and the partners who chose such arrangements were urged to be indiscreet about it and unashamed (*Taalumot Lev*, vol. 3, 32:1).

A major source of the taboo against nonmarital sex is Maimonides' ruling that it was tantamount to prostitution (*Mishnah Torah, Hilchot Ishut* 1:4). His ruling was based on a much earlier ruling by the first-century Rabbi Eliezer, whom the sages overruled when they held that a prostitute was only someone who rendered herself accessible to all, at random, and for a price (Babylonian Talmud, *Yevamot* 61b). Nachmonides further qualified the Maimonidean ruling to apply solely to casual sex, as opposed to sex in the context of a living-together relationship (*T'shuvot HaRamban*, no. 284). The rabbis in the talmudic period, however, made no such qualification and ruled that even casual sex is not considered prostitution (Babylonian Talmud, *Yevamot* 61b) and that living-together relationships are valid alternatives to marriage (Babylonian Talmud, *Sanhedrin* 21a).

Maimonides' prohibitory ruling was further codified by the *Tur*, the codes of the fourteenth-century Rabbi Yaakov ben Asher, which states: "If the couple is living together without marriage, the community should compel the man to send the woman from his home," and again in the *Shulchan Aruch*, the codes of the sixteenth-century Rabbi Yosef Karo, who states that if a couple has sex without the rite of marriage, "it is like nothing," meaning inconsequential to Jewish law. Even if their intentions were to be married through the sex act, he adds, it means nothing unless there were witnesses to that intention. Rabbi Karo then echoes the ruling of the *Tur* that if the unmarried couple is living together, the community should stop it (*Shulchan Aruch, Even HaEzer* 26:1). His contemporary, Rabbi Moshe Isserles, adds that the reason for this is: "for of course it is an embarrassment for her to immerse herself [in a public ritual pool or *mikveh* after her menstrual period, as she will be among married women and they will discover that she is single and involved sexually with a man or she'd have no cause to be there] and thus he will end up having intercourse with her while she is still in a state of *nidah*. However, if they live together and she *does* immerse herself for him, there are those authorities who permit it and this is the *pilegesh* relationship mentioned in the Torah" (*Rama* on *Shulchan Aruch, Even HaEzer* 26:1).

The seventeenth-century Rabbi Shmuel ben Uri adds his comments on the above:

> It is more probable that even according to the opinion of the *Tur* there is no prohibition against the *pilegesh* context of relationship. And what he (the *Tur*) wrote, that we compel him to send her out of his house, that is because of the fear that she would be too embarrassed to immerse. And it appears from these opinions that there is no penalty for engaging in such a relationship. That there is any kind of prohibition at any level is altogether not clear. And if you will argue "How can it be said that there is no prohibition against nonmarital sex when we have a teaching that a bride without a [marriage ritual] is forbidden sexually to the groom like a *nidah*—and the *pilegesh* is without the marriage rite?" This argument was already answered in the responsa of *Ramban*, no. 284, where he explains that the Torah only required the ritual of marriage and the seven blessings if he wishes to marry her so that they will be obligated to one another in all matters concerning husband and wife, and that she shall be forbidden to all other men. However, in the case of *pilegesh*, there is no requirement of either the seven blessings or the marital rite. . . . And it is also evident from the words of the *Rosh* (fourteenth-century Rabbi Asher ben Yechiel) that a man can fulfill the obligation to be fruitful and multiply in a nonmarital relationship. (*Beit Shmuel* on *Shulchan Aruch, Even HaEzer* 26:1)

Writes the eighteenth-century Rabbi Yaakov of Emden, whose lengthy responsum on the issue follows this chapter:

Anyone who thinks that by being in a *pilegesh* relationship one is failing to fulfull some kind of commandment to get married, is seriously in error. . . . for the Torah did not command us to marry, only to be fruitful and multiply in a permissible manner (i.e., nonadulterous, nonincestuous, and by mutual consent). And this *mitzvah* can be fulfilled also in a nonmarital relationship. But as for marriage itself, the Torah never actually obligated it. Rather, thus did She (the Torah) say: "*When* a man takes a woman to be his *wife*, only *then* is the marriage rite required, and he is then obligated to do for her as is customary for the daughters of Israel in that time. (*Sheylot Ya'avetz*, vol. 2, no. 15)

It is important to note here that the Torah's mandate to "be fruitful and multiply" applies solely to men. A woman is not required by the Torah to bear children (Babylonian Talmud, *Yevamot* 65b). The ancient rabbis also taught that a woman may drink a contraceptive potion they referred to as "the cup of roots" to sterilize herself if she so wishes (Babylonian Talmud, *Tosefta Yevamot*, chap. 8). In general, Judaism does not ask of someone something that might be life-threatening to them or dangerous to their well-being.

There are some circles within the Orthodox Jewish community that require a *gett* (ritual divorce process) from either party in a nonmarital relationship. Scanning the sources, however, it is clear that this is a minority ruling with no real halakhic basis (*Mishnah Torah, Hilchot Gerushin* 10:19; *Rama* on *Shulchan Aruch, Even HaEzer* 26:1; *Igrot Moshe, Even HaEzer,* vol. 2, no. 332; *Sheylot Ya'avetz,* vol. 2, no. 15; *T'shuvot Binyamin Z'ev,* no. 111; *T'shuvot Tashbatz,* vol. 3, no. 47; *Sheilot HaRadvaz,* no. 351 and no. 1078; *Sheylot HaRashba,* no. 1243; *T'shuvot M'il Tzedek,* no. 2; *T'shuvot Kerem Shlomo,* no. 88; *Ma'aseh Rokeach* in his commentary on *Mishnah Torah, Hilchot Ishut* 1:4). "Even according to those who do require a *gett* in these circumstances," writes Rabbi Z. Twerski, "if there is a question of the man refusing to give a *gett,* a *gett* becomes unnecessary should the woman wish to marry someone else" (*T'shuvot HaRav Tverski,* no. 15):

> If a couple has gotten married according to civil law, it is then assumed that their intention was to *not* marry according to the rites of Moses and Israel. And therefore there is no Jewishly legal marriage and the woman requires no *gett* from the man because of the principle that "the going out is in the same manner as the going in" (i.e., they used no Jewish rite going into the marriage, therefore no Jewish rite is needed for them to exit the marriage). (*Otsar HaPos'kim* on *Shulchan Aruch, Even HaEzer* 26:1)

Those who require the *gett* to terminate a nonmarital relationship base their argument on the statement in the Talmud that "A man does not intend his sexual intercourse with a woman as merely an act of licentiousness" (Babylonian Talmud, *Gitin* 73b) and that obviously his intentions were "honorable" and he wishes to marry her, which then would render the sex act as good as a marital rite. The flaw in this argument is twofold: Firstly, this particular *halakhah* clearly requires in such an instance that there be at least two religiously observant Jewish male witnesses who heard the couple declare their intention to marry and then saw them seclude themselves long enough to have engaged in sexual intercourse. Secondly, the context of the talmudic statement that "A man does not intend his sexual intercourse with a woman as merely an act of licentiousness" is referring to a situation where a man makes love to his ex-wife (*Rambam* in *Mishnah Torah, Hilchot Gitin* 10:19; *Meiri* on Babylonian Talmud, *Gitin* 73b and on *Mishnah* 7). In such a case, we might assume that their intentions were to get back together again as husband and wife; therefore, their lovemaking qualifies as a bonafide religious Jewish marital rite (Babylonian Talmud, *Ketubot* 2a), which indeed would require a *gett* were they to decide to split up again.

It is sad that the majority of single Jewish people across the denominational board today assume that their religion forbids nonmarital sexual relationships, when the fact is that it is quite liberal about this and other issues of human sexuality. What is sadder, however, is that most single Jewish people today do have sex and feel they are doing something Jewishly wrong. It is to them that the following chapter is dedicated, to open their eyes to the "other" opinions in their tradition that did not buy into the Christian values system but maintained a steadfast clarity of what is really *Jewish* and what is not. Judaism always has cherished the institution of marriage, and it certainly has been a preferred form of relationship. Nonetheless, it is important also to know that the *pilegesh* relationship is a viable alternative to marriage for those who are not ready for it or for whom it is not feasible, for whatever reasons.

As articulated in the following responsum on the issue by the eighteenth-century Rabbi Yaakov of Emden, *pilagshut* is an alternative that imbues a nonmarital relationship with sacredness and sexual reponsibility. Our age is one of rampant sexually transmitted diseases. It is also an age when a great percentage of the adult population is single due to divorce or career and academic involvement. In an age when we choose our own partners rather than having them chosen on our behalf, we are inclined to be very picky about whom we choose to marry. Often, in the process of choosing a mate of our own volition, we encounter severe, unresolved inner conflicts that need weeding out before we can negotiate a relationship with someone. As a result of these and so many other factors, many of us remain single most of our lives or at least during our most sexually prime years. To think that God expects people to suspend their burning sensuality for five, sometimes ten years until they find a suitable marriage partner is to accuse the Creator of being totally oblivious to the physical and emotional needs of the Creations. After all, the Torah was given to humans, not angels (Babylonian Talmud, *Berachot* 25b).

Probably in no other era, then, has the *pilagshut* option of relationship become more pressing than in our own, for, again, it is a context of intimate relationship outside of marriage that promotes sexual responsibility and sacredness in place of what is often random carelessness. The following chapter is the first and only known English translation of this not-so-famous responsum of Rabbi Yaakov of Emden, whose dedication to the issue and concern for the physical and emotional pain of many single people led him to devote a significant chunk of his responsa to an issue that the rabbinate both before and after his time have touched on only lightly. In so doing, he risked controversy not only among his own constituents and colleagues, but also amid the hostile anti-Judaic culture in which he lived. Nonetheless, this renowned sage spoke his mind openly, criticizing the rabbis for withholding from the people this very important information and for further perpetuating values that were more Christian than Jewish. Hopefully, we can learn today from this responsum and formulate from it our own conclusions about *pilagshut* and how to engage it for a more wholesome and enriching sex life when marriage is not practical.

3

THE CONTROVERSIAL RESPONSUM OF RABBI YAAKOV OF EMDEN ON THE ISSUE OF NONMARITAL SEX

Translator's note

This responsum might sound sexist to some readers because it addresses the male component of both marital and nonmarital relationships as the prime subject and the female party as subsidiary. This is the way the rabbis wrote back then (and some still write or teach this way, disregarding the egalitarian nature of how we define relationship these days); it was simply old patriarchal habit that meant no ill toward women, albeit it certainly contributed to the already diseased ways in which men perceived, treated, and related to women then and now. The purpose of translating this responsum is to demonstrate that there were other opinions among the traditionalists of yore concerning sex outside the context of marriage, a phenomenon not uncommon in our times and considered "sinful"—as in "living in sin"—by Christian culture and most Jews, Orthodox and not, who are unwittingly influenced more by Christianity's moral values system than Judaism's. Here, then, Rabbi Yaakov of Emden demonstrates how the Torah does not mandate marriage as license for sexual relations between a man and a woman, but offers also the alternative option of *pilagshut,* or, literally, "partial marriage." The classical English rendition of this Hebraic term is "concubinage," but a *pilegesh* is not a concubine, is not a sex slave, and may leave the relationship whenever she feels like it without any of the hassles of divorce. As Rabbi Yaakov puts it in this responsum: "As she enters the relationship, so she leaves the relationship—by verbal declaration or agreement." He nonetheless sets down rules for such a relationship—*for instance, that a rabbi be consulted to arrange it and make sure that "a special room is set aside in the man's house for her"*—and even declares the woman "a prostitute the moment she has relations with another man while living with her current lover." His rules in these regards have no unanimous premise in the sources but are based instead upon Rabbi Yaakov's own sentiments about how such a relationship ought to happen and what it implies—again, totally in line with old-hat, patriarchal, double-standard sexism. His definition of "prostitute," above, is not in agreement with all halakhic sources, past and present, and is puzzling because it does not seem consistent with what he wrote in the first part of his responsum: "a prostitute is she who has set herself up to be accessible and ready for sex with any man who happens by," which is the more common definition in the classical sources. Later in that same section, he makes this even clearer in his disagreement with one of his predecessors: "my way is very far from his way when he rules that incidental sex—even though the woman is not making herself accessible to all—renders her a prostitute, which is not my opinion at all."

It is important to note, however, that though Rabbi Emden's strict rule against simultaneous or multiple lovers is not technically a prohibition in Jewish law, his warning should nonetheless be heeded in our age when the HIV (Human Immunodeficiency Virus) is easily transmitted through heterosexual sex. For example, he writes that if the woman in a *pilegesh* relationship has sex with a man other than her live-in lover, she and her live-in lover are forbidden to have sex with each other thereafter and they need to split up. Technically, this rule would apply only to an instance of adultery which is not the case here since there is no marriage. Yet, due to the AIDS plague of our time, his stringent stance in such a situation should not be taken lightly. If either partner has had sex with someone else, they need to get tested for AIDS and to abstain from unprotected sex for as long a period as is necessary for the test to actually be effective.

The translator asks the reader to study this responsum for its value as an essential classical resource for wrestling with the halakhic implications of nonmarital sexual relationships, such as living to-gether before marriage or as an alternative to mar-riage, and to set aside the discomfort of the sexism that creeps up during its study. The sexist element, however, is also important for us to grapple with so that we might better understand some of the archaic roots of sexism in religion, how terribly wrong it feels and sounds, and how much cleaning up of it we need to do.

The Responsum of Rabbi Yaakov Emden

from Sheylot Ye'avetz, *vol. 2, no. 15*

You ask about the issue of *pilegesh* (i.e., a non-marital sexual relationship)—to which I alluded in an earlier responsum—to clarify for you if this [kind of relationship] is a definite prohibition, as it is considered by *Rambam* (twelfth-century Maimonides—Rabbi Moshe ben Maimon). And you requested also to know more clearly exactly how and what is [a situation of] *pilegesh*.

RESPONSE: I will address your last question first. Our version [of the discussion in the Talmud] is thus: "What are wives and what are *pilagshim*? Rabbi Yehudah said in the name of Rav, 'Wives [are acquired] through religious marital rites and a *ketubah* (marriage contract), and *pilagshim* without marriage and *ketubah*'" (Babylonian Talmud, *Sanhedrin*, 21a). It is also mentioned there that the sages decreed a ban on *yichud* (an unchaperoned encounter) with an unmarried woman [instituted on account of the tragic rape of Tamar, one of King David's daughters, by her stepbrother Amnon, during an unchaperoned encounter (II Sam. 13)]. I have previously written on this matter that this ban certainly does not at all apply to [the context of] *pilegesh*. For, besides the fact that we find in Scriptures [mention of *pilegesh* relationships] even after the incident concerning Tamar, how kings and great men took concubines for themselves [and were thus involved in nonmarital relationships]—we [also] find in the Talmud, in the first chapter of the tractate of *Yoma*, an account of a sage who [upon reaching a village during his sojourns] would declare [to the local single women]: "Who, amongst you, wishes to be with me for the day?" And the Talmud comments there that "he would look for someone to be with him privately" (Babylonian Talmud, *Yoma* 18b).

And although a *pilegesh* constitutes a nonmarital status in religious law, as she is without marriage, she is nonetheless forbidden to be with another man as long as she is in a private relationship with this one because of the prohibition against prostitution, which is biblical. And also to determine the parentage of each child [should she become pregnant], which is the reason she needs to wait a period of three months if she leaves the first man and chooses to marry or to live exclusively with a second. Therefore, they did definitely not decree a ban against unchaperoned involvement with an unmarried woman, except in instances when she was not in an exclusive relationship with him, so that the daughters of Israel shall not become licentious as the prostitutes and because of the incident of Amnon and Tamar. Which is not here applicable [because there is an exclusive relationship]. And we need also to conclude therefore that [sexual relations with a woman in the relationship context of] *pilegesh* would not incur the implications of premarital sexual intercourse between a ritually engaged couple, which is considered licentious because when such a couple does marry, it will be by the conditions established by the rabbis, and it is they who considered such an act as licentious if it was not performed in accordance with their established rites for marriage, [as is implied in the Talmud]: "one who marries, does so by the conditions set forth by the rabbis" (Babylonian Talmud, *Gittin* 33a). Likewise, to an instance of a *pilegesh* [relationship] there would not apply the law of "a bride without a blessing (i.e., the marriage ritual) is forbidden to her groom as a menstruating woman," which is also why they instituted in the marital blessings the blessing "and who forbade to us those [ritually] engaged to us" (Note: In ancient times, and even today among the ultra-Orthodox, becoming engaged to marry entailed a prenuptial ritual ceremony that bound the couple to one another, short of consummation, as man and wife, replete with all related legal implications, including marital fidelity and, consequently, adultery, and requiring a divorce-like ceremonial in event of termination)—all this for the same reason [of "one who marries, does so by the conditions set forth by the rabbis"].

And all of this is not applicable but for one who takes a complete wife, through whom he benefits legally in four ways, and she through him in ten ways. And therefore does he need to engage her in accordance with the ordinances established by the sages [because each is bound to the other with certain legal responsibilities, certain expectations of obligations to and from one another] with ritual marital ceremonial. Unlike as with a *pilegesh*, who—as the term connotes—is but *p'lag ishah*, half wife, for whom such ordinances were not decreed because she lives with him without marriage or *ketubah* but is in an exclusive relationship with him for a certain time and for certain benefits, all of which are determined between the two of them. This is the way the matter appears to me. But nevertheless her legal status is as that of a single woman in all circumstances, and all this when they live together in an exclusive relationship. . . .

However, the *Ramma* (sixteenth-century Rabbi Moshe Isserles) writes in his work that the *pilegesh* [form of relationship] was *permitted only for a king, but not for a commoner*. And it is not known from what kind of source is this new concept known. For it appears that it is contrary to what is revealed in the Scriptures, [where *pilegesh* relationships are associated also with men who were not kings]. Nor have we found any precedence for his view in the Talmud or in rabbinic writings. And it seems to me that he relies on the mention in the Talmud of prominent men being considered as kings in terms of their being known by the masses, whereas a layman would not be known by the masses, and that those mentioned in Scriptures as being with a *pilegesh* were men of prominent stature, and who were thus known to the public. And [,further, the *Ramma* probably also based his ruling on the opinion that] they would enter into seclusion with her but that they did not have sexual intercourse with her. And even if this is indeed so, that according to the rabbis [of the Talmud] it is forbidden [unless he is a public figure], we would have no proof from these instances, [for they speak of engaging in transient relationships, such as during travels away from places of residence, situations in which sexual liaisons could result in offspring of different geographical locations who might one day marry one another, unaware that they share the same father, which is why such relationships might only have been permitted to public figures]. And it is because of the ban of Rabbi Eliezer [that "one should not marry a woman in one place and marry another in a second place lest the world be filled with immorality, for then shall a brother marry a sister"] that they ruled so, which is not relevant to a situation where there is an exclusive *pilegesh* relationship in his place of residence, in which case the relationship would certainly be public knowledge in all regard. And thus there would be no issue of "lest a brother marry his sister, and a father his daughter."

Moreover, I have found, in the course of my bibliographic search, the responsa of *Ramban* (Rabbi Moshe ben Nakhmon), where he challenges the ruling of *Rambam* (Maimonides) *on* this subject and where he replies to his inquirer as follows, and these are his words: "I do not know why there is any question about [the permissibility of a *pilegesh* relationship], for she is certainly permissible because she is in an exclusive relationship with him. Casual sex, after all, was not forbidden but by the teaching of Rabbi Eliezer [that a man should not have a relationship with different women in separate locations, etc.] But if he brings her into his home and she is exclusively with him, and thus her children would be known to him and are called by his name, she is permitted, for King David [engaged in such relationships] and we do not find anywhere, not in Scripture and not in the Talmud, any distinction between a king and a commoner regarding this matter. And we indeed find that the great men of Israel [engaged in such relationships]. And if you will argue that the Judges were considered as kings, then you thereby support by your own words the permissibility [of such relationships] to the spiritual masters. . . ."

Now, even though *Ramban* supports my con-
tention and I have shared his conclusions on the
issue, it will not satisfy us that he brought proof from
the fact that King David engaged in such relationships, for from King David and from the ancient
Judges of Israel we have no proof because they were
around prior to the ban against unchaperoned en-
counters with single women, which was not enacted
until after the incident of Amnon and Tamar, and
pilegesh relationships continued nevertheless afterward. And because it was always permissible, it remained permissible and was not included in the ban.
Rather, [*Ramban*] should have brought his proof from
the grandson of King Rehoboam, [who reigned several generations after King David and thus after the
incident of Amnon and Tamar, when the ban was
already in force]. And still this sort of proof would be
up for question by those who remain skeptical [about
the permissibility of *pilegesh*], for just because these
post-Davidic kings did so does not mean they necessarily did the right thing. And that which *Ramban*
writes—"you thereby support by your own words the
permissibility for the spiritual masters"—puzzles me,
for how can such a great rabbi have overlooked
the talmudic ruling that it is unquestionably permissible for a prominent sage due to his exposure to the
public?

Nevertheless, I rejoice in the fact that further
reading of [*Ramban's*] teaching on the matter bears

out a conclusion synonymous with my own: that it is completely permissible. He continues as follows: "And lest you claim that it may be permissible by biblical law but prohibited by rabbinic law, where in the Talmud was such a decree recorded? And in what period did this law change [from being permissible to becoming forbidden]?" And it is important to note that what he writes thereafter—that "if he wished to be [in a *pilegesh* relationship] so that she is not bound to him and is therefore not forbidden to other men, then he has that option"—should not be misconstrued to mean that she may be with other men while she is already in a relationship with someone. God forbid to attribute such a notion to the [*Ramban*]. For she is certainly forbidden to any other man so long as she is already in a special relationship with someone. And if she renders herself accessible to anyone, then she certainly becomes like a prostitute, [which is forbidden]. Rather, [*Ramban's*] intent, when he wrote about her not being forbidden to other men, was that if she were to leave him, she would not require a *gett* (ritual divorce), [unlike] a married woman, who is free to be with another man only if she acquires a *gett* and who, if she failed to get divorced first, remains married as before, even though she has left her husband. Whereas, concerning [a woman in a *pilegesh* relationship], the moment she ceases cohabitation with the one she was with, the prohibition [against her being with another] is lifted and she may marry or live with another man by word alone (i.e., without any document declaring her marital status). And by the mere act of her leaving his house and no longer sleeping with him, she automatically resumes her status as a single woman after waiting the three-month period [for determining parentage in case she is pregnant]. So in virtually all matters of the ruling on this issue have I concurred with the masterful *Ramban*, except in the matter of reconciling this ruling on the issue with that of *Rambam*. And that which *Ramban* writes—that even according to *Rambam* there would be no clear prohibition against a *pilegesh* relationship for a commoner, that even in his Laws of Kings he does not state that it is permissible only to a king—puzzles me greatly because he clearly spells out the permission for a king and the prohibition for a commoner. Perhaps *Ramban* was in possession of a version of *Rambam* different from ours.

Nonetheless, this ruling, which *Rambam* introduced anew from his own mind, [that the *pilegesh* relationship is allowed only to a king] must have come to him through some kind of prophecy, it seems, because if it is indeed as he says, where do we find anything like it, that something that was generally prohibited was, however, permitted to a king? Besides the fact that *pilegesh* was never forbidden in the first place but, on the contrary, was permitted in the Scriptures. On the other hand, we find that, quite to the contrary, the law was far more stringent for a king than for a commoner, and specifically in regards to the related issue of marriage, in which kings were forbidden to have more than eighteen wives, whereas anyone else was allowed to have as many as they could properly care for. Nor were kings allowed to have excess of horses, or of gold and silver, etc. (Deut. 17:16–17), whereas no such limitations were placed on commoners. In my commentary on *Rambam* (*Mishnah Torah, Hilchot Ishut*, pt. I), I wrestled with the issue on [*Ramban's*] behalf and set it straight for him. And these are the words of *Rambam* there: "Therefore, one who has casual sex with a woman— that is, without marriage—deserves to be flogged, for he has had intercourse as with a prostitute." And on this statement, [*Ramban*] challenges him and argues: "A prostitute is only someone who renders herself accessible to all men, etc." And about that I wrote how I did not feel that there was any dispute, for *Rambam* also held that a prostitute is only a woman who renders herself accessible to all (*Mishnah Torah, Hilchot Na'arah B'tulah*, end of chap. 2). But there are other questions he asks about the implications of *Rambam*'s statement [,such as: If a woman who engages in casual sex is indeed considered as a prostitute,] why would a man be required to pay a fine to a father for seducing his [minor] daughter? But this, too, presents no difficulty because of what we have established: that a prostitute is she who has set herself up to be accessible and ready for sex with any man who happens by—exactly what *Rambam* clarifies at the end of the second chapter

of the Laws of the Young Virgin. The Torah's institution of fines rather than flogging for the seduction
of a young maiden thus applies to a situation where
the resulting sex act occurred in the moment, just that
once, and without the knowledge of her father, and
where the girl was not set up for it, which would be
highly unusual and is rarely to be found. However, if
a father did set up his virgin daughter to have sex with
anyone, he causes the land to be filled with evil. And
one who does set up his daughter to that, she becomes a prostitute and both parties to the sex act are
liable for flogging. And it is clear in this law that such
would not apply to one who was seduced, where she
was thus not open and ready for the act but had to
be talked into it.

But concerning the issue of *pilegesh*, there is
conflict in opinion, for there *Rambam* prohibits it
for a commoner and *Rabad* (twelfth-century Rabbi
Abraham Ibn Daud) permits it to all in the context of
an exclusive relationship. [And perhaps *Rambam*
permitted it to a king alone because among commoners she might become as a sex object, moving from
living with one to living with another and for sex
alone, whereas a king's concubine becomes forbidden to anyone else and remains in an exclusive relationship with the king at all times, and is prohibited
to anyone else under pain of death even after the king
has died or if the king sends her away, and she is even
then permitted only to the king's successor. And it is
thus that *Rambam* had no difficulty with the fact that

the Judges of Israel or prominent religious leaders engaged in *pilegesh* relationships because he considered them as kings, who would not abuse this sort of context of relationship, as commoners would be more prone to do. And as the Talmud teaches: "Sons of the sages are as the sons of the kings" (Babylonian Talmud, *Semakhot*, chap. 3). And that is perhaps the reasoning behind *Rambam*'s ruling on *pilegesh*.]

Rabad, however, did reason thus but ruled that because *pilegesh* had been permitted, it had been permitted to all men because we do not find a prohibition against it delineated in the Torah. And he felt that in the context of exclusive relationship, she would be sufficiently protected from becoming licentious. And I found in the responsa of the *Radvaz* (fifteenth-century Rabbi Dovid Ibn Zimra) where he reasons on the issue of *pilegesh* as I have on behalf of the *Rambam*'s ruling and distinguishes between incidental sex and sexual intercourse in the context of an exclusive relationship (*Rishonot*, no. 225). However, my way is very far from his way when he rules that incidental sex—even though the woman is not making herself accessible to all—renders her a prostitute, which is not my opinion at all. Also not of my opinion is his new decree that *Rambam*'s restriction of *pilegesh* for a king only is because the sages ordained it so, lest she would be too embarrassed to immerse herself ritually (following menstruation) for a commoner, whereas she would not be embarrassed to do so for a king or leader. I do not agree with him on that, and who would indeed pay heed to him on that matter, for there is no flavor or fragrance to this line of reasoning, nor evidence of any substance.

And regarding the argument of the decree against unchaperoned liaison with a single woman, this is certainly a fence to protect values of the Torah, for two reasons: either to prevent forbidden intimacy or—worse yet—because of the prohibition against sexual contact with a menstruating woman [or a woman who has not performed ritual immersion since her last period]. Because she is not in an exclusive relationship with him, she will not have immersed by the time they find themselves in spontaneous contact. And by then, the fires of her passion have already been aroused and there is no time for immersion. And if you will say that this does not render her a prostitute because it was a spur-of-the-moment, incidental act, which is not considered prostitution, the sages nonetheless might have feared that a single woman could find this spontaneity favorable and end up allowing herself to be seduced by one man after another and thus become a prostitute, which is forbidden by the Torah both for her and for anyone who has sex with her in that context. But this is inapplicable to the situation of *pilegesh* (a committed, nonmarital relationship), for she is exclusively in relationship with a man, and in such a context did the sages not ever ban the unchaperoned liaison with a single woman, just like they did not ban unchaperoned liaison with the woman one is married to; there is no difference between this one and that one because both are permitted to him. And according to the simple meaning of the Torah law regarding these matters, the *pilegesh* has no more a reason to be embarrassed about immersing in the public *mikveh* (ritual pool) than the married woman. And we have no right to issue some new decree that it is embarrassing for a nonmarried woman to immerse in the public *mikveh* [and that a nonmarital relationship should therefore be forbidden]. For if you do so, you will also bring ill-repute upon the saintly ones of ancient times [who were engaged in such relationships], and not only upon those mentioned in the Scriptures—which account for a period during which the *pilegesh* relationship was commonplace and fully honored and acceptable—but also upon the rabbis recorded in the Talmud, who were known to engage in such relationships, such as the Talmud's mention of the rabbis who would engage women to be with them for a day during their visit to a village (Babylonian Talmud, *Yoma* 18b), and certainly it was without marriage rites or a *ketubah* (marriage contract), as it is said there, and there was no question about it.

Moreover, *Radbaz*, in his responsum on the issue, further writes: "And know that even *Ramban*, who permits *pilegesh* relationship, if he were to live in our times, he would forbid it because of the sexual licentiousness that prevails now. And thus did *Ramban* add to his responsum: 'And you, O rabbi, in your place you ought to warn your people against the *pilegesh* relationship because if they knew that it was permitted, they would engage licentiously in sexual activity and would end up having sex with women who are yet in their menstrual states. . . .'"

And this is the additional text that *Radbaz* published on his own and attributed to the responsum of Nakhmonides in order to forbid the *pilegesh* relationship and to construct a fence around it, something that was unheard of until then. In fact, he went contrary to his own reasoning because to allow alternative options of sexual relationships that are not in violation of Torah principles, would—on the contrary—reduce, not increase, sexual immorality. For there is no comparison between the choices of one who has bread in his basket and one who hasn't (i.e., people who have options available to them will be less likely to take their passions beyond moral expression). Indeed, we find that the sages often permitted that which was ordinarily forbidden by them in circumstances that did not violate Torah principle. Not only that, but in some situations they declared that it is better even for a colleague to trespass a secondary prohibition than to otherwise end up trespassing a major one. . . . And here we are dealing with an issue about which there is no prohibition—[not by the rabbis,] not even by the Torah. And it is an issue that even if it arose upon the mind, as it arose in the mind of Maimonides, that there is some reason to suspect that it might be forbidden, nonetheless, in our time it would be appropriate to permit it because of the much greater evil that would result from withholding such permission. . . . As the *Radbaz* himself admits, people are trespassing boundaries in sexual morality, and this is certainly so also in our time and in all places because the door of permissibility has been shut in front of their faces. Because if the people knew that the *pilegesh* relationship was allowed, they would definitely not be stumbling over serious trespasses of sexual morality. It therefore seems to me that we ought to be teaching in public that a person is allowed to be in a *pilegesh* relationship, in order to rescue them from serious violations that are occurring daily. And definitely will people desist from severe transgressions, such as sexual intimacy with a woman who is married or who is in her menstrual state, or with prostitutes, or with daughters of other religions. Nor will they come to waste seed. And why should we continue to impose this prohibition without cause, to place such stumbling blocks that are based upon and perpetuated by a stringent ruling that has absolutely no premise to support it? And "is it not enough what the Torah has forbidden, that we need to add further prohibitions?" (Jerusalem Talmud, *Nedarim* 9:1 [25a]). . . .

. . . Bottom line, all the early authorities agree on the issue that the *pilegesh* relationship is permitted. And though they might also have seen the negative opinion of Maimonides, it did not affect their rulings because they had no idea what his premise was for forbidding it, completely contrary to the scriptural evidence permitting it. Also, all of the latter-day authorities in *halakhah* were silent about this subject, and their silence about it is tantamount to their admission and decision concerning its permissibility. And even according to those who prohibited it, their ruling is nothing but some brand-new decree invented from their hearts and without root or substance. It therefore appears to me that we ought to pay no mind to the conclusion of the *Radbaz*, who forbids the *pilegesh* relationship based on a responsum of the *Rash* (fourteenth-century Rabbeinu Asher) regarding a woman who was hired to tend to the house of a man who then engaged her in sexual relations. There, the *Rash* ruled that the rabbinic court may compel him to dismiss her from his home because it is known that she will be embarrassed to immerse. And *Radbaz* comments on this: "If *pilegesh* is permitted, why do we compel him to dismiss her from his home?" But the *Rash* is correct in his ruling because she is not in a relationship with this man but is in his hire for the expressed purpose of tending to his house, and he is taking sexual liberties with her. It is obvious, then, that she is not a *pilegesh* but is being treated like a prostitute, which is forbidden, and there is no way to determine seed from seed, [and it can lead to brother marrying sister because there is no clarity of parentage if she were to become pregnant]. And he will be violating the prohibition against sex with a menstruant woman because she is certainly embarrassed to be seen immersing, as she is not known to be in any *pilegesh* relationship at the time and she is not in an exclusive relationship with him, nor does he desire her as a partner other than a means of satisfying his lust in a wrongful manner, like the sweetness of stolen water (Prov. 9:17). So we must here certainly rule that he is forced to send her away, which is not the case with a *pilegesh* who—from the very start—would be specifically and knowingly involved with him for the purpose of intimate relationship and therefore have no cause for embarrassment when she immerses following her period, just like a wife, because she is with him permissibly. . . . I am appalled at such a great rabbi like *Radbaz* that he would lump a housekeeper in the same category as *pilegesh*! Does it sound reasonable that when a man hires a woman to keep house for him that it is then also assumed that she will be his lover? Who ever heard of such a thing? Rather, *pilegesh* is a publicly known situation and she is in an indiscreet and exclusive relationship [with whomever she is with at the time], and there is no issue of adultery, as there would be with someone else's wife. . . . and her children maintain full claims to the lineage of the man who fathered them. . . . and we do not have to worry about illicit relations during the menstrual state because she has no reason to be embarrassed to immerse. . . . and so on. There is therefore not so much as a hint of any prohibition whatsoever against the *pilegesh* relationship in the responsum of the *Rash*. In fact, he does not particularly reveal where his opinion leans on the subject, whether to the side of Maimonides or to that of his opponents. And it is more likely that we can join him to the side of those who permit it than to consider him silent on the matter altogether.

After I had written all that appears to me regarding this issue, I thought that I had fulfilled my obligations concerning all this, to establish the *halakhah* and decision that the *pilegesh* relationship is permitted. But then came to me the responsum of *Rivash* (fourteenth-century Rabbi Yitzchak ben Sheishet), and behold he stands against me with the appearance of a brazen warrior of wisdom, reinvigorating the force of stringency, to strongly forbid [*pilegesh*]. And I am forced to examine also his words before I can arrive at a conclusive chapter to this matter, to see what root is to be found [in his argument], unto which to add or from which to detract something about this subject. [Most of his arguments parallel those of others with whom we have already dealt above. But his main argument is that *pilegesh* is a single woman, and unchaperoned liaisons with single women were banned by the court of King David after the rape of David's daughter Tamar by her half-brother Amnon]. . . . But the *pilegesh* is not like the single woman with whom the ban against unchaperoned liaison applies. [*Pilegesh*] means *p'lag ishah* (partial wife), and she is like a single woman only in regards to her not requiring a *gett* (ritual divorce) and that one who has sex with her while she is in relationship with another is not committing adultery and thus not liable for capital punishment, albeit he is violating the prohibition against prostitution (Rabbi Emden's opinion—not necessarily everyone's definition of prostitution).

He also writes that because the ban against unchaperoned liaison with a single woman was established by the court of King David, there is therefore no mention of *pilegesh* relationships from King David's time and on except in Solomon's household. Thus his proof that the ban concerning single women applied to the *pilegesh* as well. However, it must have slipped by him that Rehoboam, [who lived several generations after David], had sixty *pilagshim*. . . . The *pilegesh* is not fully a single woman but half a wife, and because she is permitted to live with a man according to the Torah, it is then clear that when she ceases to live with him, she returns to the full status of the single woman she was before. This is like the married woman who, as she entered the marriage with a document, so she leaves the marriage with a document. So with the *pilegesh*: As she entered the relationship by living with him, so does she end the relationship by not living with him and by removing the exclusive nature of the relationship at the end of whatever time period that was mutually agreed upon by both parties, or because she wishes to leave him, or because she had sex with another man while still living with the first, or if he abused her or did not uphold whatever they agreed between each other.

In such circumstances she simply leaves him; as she came in by word, she leaves by word. And she does not have to uncover her head in the marketplace (i.e., publicize her single status), for that is forbidden for Jewish women, even single women, as Maimonides writes. (Note: Since Emden's day, single women have over time stopped covering their heads in the Orthodox community, and even many married women have done the same in the more modern Orthodox communities.) Rather, it is through the removal of the exclusive nature of their relationship alone that the bonds of *pilagshut* are severed. And there is no licentiousness in this, for we apply the principle "the way she came in is the way she goes out" also to a *pilegesh*. . . .

. . . My master Rabbi Chaim ruled that *pilegesh* is permissible but that such a relationship prevents a man from fulfilling the obligation of marriage. I do not agree with him on this point. Rather, I say that marriage is one thing and *pilagshut* is another, and both are options permitted by the Torah. So if a man wishes to marry a woman completely, to benefit through her in various ways, and she, too, wishes to merit the many benefits of marriage, and thereby he will be barred from [ever marrying] her close relatives and she from his, and anyone who has sex with her will be liable for the death penalty, then [—if this is what two people want—] the Torah mandated specifically that they perform the marital rite. And if a couple preferred to be in a *pilagshut* form of relationship because it suited them better, perhaps because the man already has a wife but needs someone who would help out with the family and be his lover as well because his wife is not always able to be with him sexually, such as during her period or when he is traveling, or perhaps because he is not married and does not wish to be bound by the weighty responsibilities of marriage; and the woman, too, prefers this form of relationship to marriage so that if the man mistreats her, she can simply leave the relationship instantly, without the hassles of acquiring a *gett* from him in accordance with all the intricate details this involves, and by simply leaving him she is free of him in so light a manner; or perhaps they do not wish to be barred from each other's close relations after they have separated—in any event, both parties might then prefer the *pilegesh* relationship to a marital one. For this reason did the Torah also present the Israelites with the *mitzvah* (sacred instruction) of the *pilegesh* relationship, which is initiated by word and ended by word. Thus do we derive from what the Torah has revealed to us in principle that it is completely permitted but it is not an obligation, but then neither is marriage an obligation, as we discussed earlier—only a precious form of *mitzvah*. But certainly the *pilegesh* relationship is a permissible option, and for those who need it, the Torah was lenient about it and did not require the marital rite. Nonetheless, exclusive living-together is required (Note: Rabbi Emden's own opinion, which he repeats throughout this responsum without any sources or premises other than the fear that if the woman sleeps with another man while living with someone, we won't know who the father is if there is a child involved, and this, in turn, later can lead to siblings of different fathers marrying one another), and that the man not treat her lightly and allow other men to be intimate with her, for against such a thing did the Torah warn: "There shall not be a prostitute from among the daughters of Israel and the land shall not be filled with immorality" (Lev. 19:29 and Deut. 23:18) because the children born of random sexual liaisons with many partners will not know their parentage. It is clear, then, that if there is no cause for such concerns—as the children of the *pilegesh* are known to their father and claim full inheritance rights like the children of a married woman—such a form of relationship was permitted by the Torah to an Israelite as well as to a Noahide (non-Jew). And because this is not an obligatory *mitzvah* but a voluntary one, it was not articulated among the "Thou Shalts" of the Torah's instructions. And its laws are known and assumed upon humankind since the human was first placed upon the earth, and thus there is no commandment mandating that a man take unto himself a *pilegesh* as there is concerning a wife, which is a clearly stated *mitzvah*—albeit the kind that is obligatory only when it occurs, such as with the *mitzvah* of *tzitzit* (fringes) [that are knotted on a four-cornered garment, providing one has a four-cornered garment to begin with, but one isn't obligated to go out and acquire one. Likewise, the Torah does not say that a man must marry, but "When a man takes a woman to wife . . ." (Deut. 22:14 and 24:1). A man is not required to marry, in other words, but if he decides to, the laws are such and such]. And [because the *pilegesh* form of relationship was an established, ancient form,] the Torah had to delineate the laws of being with a woman in such a way that was outside the realm of the then standard nonmarital *pilegesh* way. And so marriage was a new law instituted by the Torah after it was given to the people, to direct them in how to do marriage versus *pilagshut*, a set of laws involving conditions for the Jewish couple desiring to be in a marriage with one another. And the option of *pilagshut* was left for us from among the customs of our ancestors and the early [pre-Sinai] holymen of our people.

And along this line, we rebut what the *Rivash* claimed, that to be in a *pilegesh* relationship would mean that one would be delinquent in fulfilling the obligation to be married and that even if a man is in a relationship with one hundred women, he would still be obligated to be in marriage with each of them. . . . which is a totally erroneous argument . . . for it is not like donning a four-cornered garment without any *tzitzit* on it, but rather like wearing any number of garments that do not have four corners on them and thus not being obligated to tie *tzitzit* on them nor being thereby delinquent in fulfilling the *mitzvah* of *tzitzit* (Num. 15:38). Even according to the opinion that *tzitzit* is obligatory in itself [and one who has no four-cornered garment is obliged to acquire one for the purpose of donning *tzitzit*], one needs to possess but a single garment with *tzitzit* to fulfill the *mitzvah*. Likewise regarding our subject matter, albeit even less so, for the Torah did not require outright that we marry, only that we "be fruitful and multiply" (Genesis 1:22 and 9:1) through legitimate means, and although this is a clear mandate in the Torah, it can be accomplished just as well in a *pilegesh* relationship. But marriage with a woman is not an outright requirement in itself; rather, the Torah words it thus: "When a man takes a wife . . ." then he must fulfill specific responsibilities to her as is befitting [wives]. And I have not found so much as a hint in the Torah that for a man to be with a woman he must necessarily marry her. Only, if he desires to take to himself a woman who would belong to him completely as his wife, then he had to fulfill the requirements that the Torah instituted for the relationship context of marriage, and in that context he can fulfill the *mitzvah* of marriage, just as he would fulfill the *mitzvah* of wearing *tzitzit*, for which, too, he [performs a specific rite and] recites a special prayer [even though he is not obligated to perform this *mitzvah* unless he happens to own a four-cornered garment]. . . . And it is akin to any of the other *mitzvot* in the Torah that are not mandatory, whose fulfillment is required only if situations arise where one is engaged in that particular *mitzvah*, not that one is obligated to create the situation in order to fulfill the *mitzvah*. So it is with the *mitzvah* of marriage.

. . . Further, *Rivash* argues that *pilegesh* is forbidden by Maimonides, who forbade sexual relations with a woman if the intention is not for marriage, but the *pilegesh* relationship is not necessarily nonmarital in the sense that it [is a committed relationship between two people and is therefore] included in the concept of marriage. And thus do we find quite often in the *t'nakh* (Scriptures) that the *pilegesh* was referred to as "wife," and in the Torah, too, for instance, where it is written: "And Abraham took a wife and her name was Keturah" (Gen. 25:1), yet we find in the Book of Chronicles: "And Keturah was the *pilegesh* of Abraham" (I Chron. 1:32). For the *pilegesh* is nevertheless part wife, though she is not as a married woman nor completely as a single woman but a bit of both . . .

. . . And about his argument that if a man lives with a woman in a nonmarital relationship it is considered like they are fully married because "A man does not intend his sexual intercourse to be casual" (Babylonian Talmud, *Gittin* 81b) [i.e., his intention must have been for the woman to become his wife], I have already responded to this above, let alone that it is clear from the Talmud that such intention needs to be openly articulated and that the woman must know that it is the man's intention that they be married through their sexual union, that it is with those specifics that they become married, for she does not acquiesce for the sake of random sex but for the sake of marriage, and that agreement on both their parts makes the marriage. Certainly does his intercourse with her in such a circumstance become prostituted if his intentions turn out not to be for the sake of marrying her thereby. But what evidential relevance does this have with two people who engage regularly in sexual relations exclusively with one another and with mutual consent?—something that the Torah permitted without any reservation. . . . Rather, it seems that alongside every one of his arguments sits the rebuttal to it, and for every source he brings that forbids, there is one just as authoritative that permits. . . . It is appalling that *Rivash* invested so much time and effort in trying to prove something as forbidden when it has been permitted by the elders who preceded him across many generations. For even he himself admits that in Spain the practice of *pilegesh* is widespread, and indiscreetly so. And yet there is not a single one of the great rabbinic leaders through the generations who has found it worthy of any concern. On the contrary, it would seem more beneficial to codify [the permissibility of the *pilegesh* relationship] as *halakhah* (Jewish law) and to sound the announcement in a place of integrity, to declare a solid ruling for now and for future generations that the *pilegesh* relationship is completely permitted. And there is also nothing new about it, for all we will be doing is rendering permissible that which has already always been permissible. And even a prophet is not allowed to innovate a new commandment and add a prohibition to what the Torah has already proscribed, unless it is to protect the principles of the Torah herself. Indeed, we have witnessed how the early sages have been known to innovate decrees and stringencies, for we are instructed by the Torah to create observances that would preserve her precepts (Lev. 18:30 and Babylonian Talmud, *Mo'ed Katan* 5a). Nevertheless, we have never witnessed, nor have our ancestors told us, nor have our sages informed us that it ever arose in their minds to innovate a prohibition against the *pilegesh* relationship. Rather, we have known only the opposite.

Yet, it behooves us first to examine thoroughly the nature of the *pilegesh* relationship before we go about spreading its permissibility, in order that its practice be free of any possible violation that might result in the process. Firstly—even though it was never prohibited by a majority rule, but, on the contrary, its acceptance was widespread—we need to explore whether the Ban of Rabbeinu Gershom (eleventh century) [against bigamy] would be applicable insofar that a man who is already married to someone would then not be permitted to be in a *pilegesh* relationship with another woman. Secondly, we need to deal with the principle "Matters that are permissible, but the local custom is to consider them forbidden, you do not have the right to treat as permissible in front of them" (Jerusalem Talmud, *Pesachim*

4). And thirdly, perhaps we ought to forbid it . . . on the premise of those who forbade the permitted out of fear that the ignorant and the nonobservant would be thereby led to actual transgressions, such as sexual relations during the woman's menstrual state.

In regards to the first question, concerning the Ban of Rabbeinu Gershom, aside from the fact that his decree was not accepted in all lands, nor by all Jewish communities, for it never applied at all to the communities of the east or the west, only in the Germanic empire alone, and, moreover, it was influenced by the prevailing morals of the [Christians], who forbade a man from having more than one wife and even considered such a thing akin to adultery, and [so the Jewish ban against bigamy is a result of our having become assimilated among the non-Jewish nations, and] it is therefore more the reason to abrogate the decree [because it was influenced by a values system alien to our own]. But did they not also say [about the ban] that it was decreed only until the end of the 5000th (thus terminating in the Hebraic year of 5,000, or 1240 c.e.)? Moreover, [Rabbeinu Gershom's decree] must not be in violation of the commandment "You shall not add [to the laws of the Torah]" (Deut. 4:2 and 13:1), and a new decree leaves nothing to interpretation but what the text specifies, [and in the Ban of Rabbeinu Gershom, the text reads] only that it is forbidden for a man to engage a second wife while still married to the first. Thus, [based on the literal implication of the text], the ban was not considered applicable . . . to a situation of *yivum* [the Torah-mandated automatic marriage of a man—whether already married—to the widow of his brother if his brother died childless (Deut. 25:5), in order to bring children into the world on behalf of his deceased brother].

With a *pilegesh*, too, a man can fulfill the *mitzvah* of bringing children into the world in a situation where he cannot find a woman who will marry him. Or perhaps he is married already but to a woman who cannot bear children, and he is not able to divorce her either because of the strong bond between them or because her *ketubah* is worth more than he can afford (Note: In addition to being a ritual marriage contract, the *ketubah* also stipulates the amount of financial resources the husband pledges to his wife in the event that the marriage is terminated).

In regards to the second issue, the principle of "Matters that are permissible but the local custom is to consider them forbidden, you do not have the right to treat as permissible in front of them" applies only . . . to a practice of a prohibition around a matter that is nonetheless known to all as permissible but is observed as a prohibition only as a safeguard around something else that indeed is forbidden by the Torah. But neither qualification relates to the issue of *pilegesh*, for it has already been explained that the *pilegesh* relationship was never forbidden at all by any majority rule, nor was it ever known to have been accepted as a proscription. On the contrary, the majority permitted it, and the words of the single one who forbade it, based on his reading of Maimonides' code, are nullified by the fact that his argument has no fuel to combust it.

And regarding the fact that our communities have refrained from the practice of the *pilegesh* option of relationship, they have done so of their own volition and out of their assumption that it is prohibited. And the principle is that a custom based on erroneous assumption is not considered a custom (Babylonian Talmud, *Sofrim* 14). And we inform them that it is permissible if their custom is based on the assumption that it is forbidden. And the truth is that [the *pilegesh* option of relationship] is permissible and no prohibition was ever enacted against it, even as a safeguard. It is only out of lack of knowledge that it is considered as forbidden, or perhaps the community rabbi has ruled against it, which, too, is a mistake. Bottom line, the prohibition is nonextant, not even as a safeguard. On the contrary, [the option of] *pilagshut* itself is a safeguard around the Torah because it can keep one far from the commission of such wrongs as irresponsible sexuality and prostitution, and sexual liaisons with [women of spirit paths that run counter to those of Judaism], and sex [with one's wife] during the menstrual phase, and the wasting of seed [through masturbation] by men who are not married, and also by those who are married, during the period when their wives are not available to them.

[Moreover, the option of *pilagshut* is beneficial] also toward the fulfillment of the great positive *mitzvah* of bringing children into the world, [a *mitzvah*] that many times eludes even those who are married, on account of their ties to one woman alone. And thus no other people is more fitted for marriages with many women than the holy nation. Therefore did the Torah allow the Israelite man to be with many wives because he is forbidden from illicit sex (adultery and incest) and prostitution. Also, his wife, too, is forbidden to him over extended periods of time during her menstrual period or during other flows [from the womb] and after she has given birth [until her staining ceases]. And in order for him to persevere during such times, the Torah did not permit him more than one wife for naught. And also that he might increase the Jewish population. And the reasoning behind the law that [some of] the nations have instituted against polygamy is because without such a law, each country would become populated beyond what that country can accommodate for its existence. And it would be appropriate to remove the ban [of Rabbeinu Gershom] against marriage to more than one woman for a Jewish man on the basis of "And in their ways you shall not walk" (Lev. 18:3). But perhaps Rabbeinu Gershom felt compelled to institute his ban, even though it was counter to Torah law . . . because it had become life-threatening for Jews who lived among the uncircumcised [an indirect reference to the Christians] to be married to more

than one woman. And therefore I am not in agreement with what Rabbeinu Nissim (fourteenth century)
wrote in a responsum, that members of communities affected by the Ban of Rabbeinu Gershom were
duty-bound to observe that ban regardless of whether
they remained in those communities, implying that
a Jewish man from the empire of Germany who re-
located elsewhere was still bound by the ban. But in
truth it is not so because Rabbeinu Gershom did not
come to create this decree but on account of the
danger posed by the uncircumcised. Whereas in a
place where the Gentiles are not concerned about
whether a man has more than one wife, Rabbeinu
Gershom would certainly not have instituted his ban,
adding thereby to Torah law without an appropriate
premise such as a safeguard to the Torah herself. On
the contrary, [rather than a safeguard, such a decree
would be] a detriment, contributing to the neglect of
bringing children into the world and to the minimi-
zation of the sacred seed (i.e., the Jewish populace),
God forbid! Therefore, there is no doubt that Rabbeinu Gershom arrived at this decree out of a compelling need and the requirement of the hour . . .
which is inapplicable in a place where there is no
danger from the [non-Jewish] peoples there. And this
is simple and obvious.

And with regard to the third concern, [that at
times the sages declared] the permissible forbidden
to those who are unlearned in the ways of Torah . . .
but that was in situations where there were no rab-

bis to guide the unlearned and see to it that they did things right. Whereas our situation is that, though there are indeed unlearned people in our generation, nevertheless disciples of Torah dwell among them in all these places, and the Talmud and the codes of Jewish law have become widely accessible and everyone follows [their counsel and instructions]. And thus there is no cause for concern whatsoever, as I have elaborated regarding a similar matter (in *Mor U'ktziah, Orach Chayyim*, no. 453).

Moreover, the rabbi did not seem concerned about the stringent practice of women who wait forty days before performing ritual immersion after birthing a boy and eighty days after birthing a girl, [thereby delaying also the resumption of physical intimacy with their husbands]. While he wrote numerous reasons for perpetuating it, he made no effort to abrogate it on the basis that it is not a permanent custom. And my father, my teacher, the wise one, takes him to task in his book (*Chakham Tz'vi*, no. 8), and we know that [my father] abolished this abhorrent custom in his community and instructed women not to delay their ritual immersion [beyond the time when their postpartum healing has completed]. And this edict did the women in his community follow, according to what my father spoke, for he realized that this was a stringent practice that would only lead too easily to actual transgression [on account of the lengthy period of abstinence that would result].

And so, regarding these rabbis who follow in the Ashkenazic (Germanic, Western European) customs, it would have been better had they never existed and had they never been created in this land, for they have wrought all sorts of destructive stumbling blocks upon the people, compelling many to transgress what is indeed forbidden by the Torah [in their attempts to create safeguards around what is not at all forbidden by the Torah]. Therefore, in my opinion, it is a great *mitzvah* to publicize that [*pilagshut*] is permitted. Especially is this so in our generation, when the "Canaanites" dwell in the land who so love sexual licentiousness—in particular, the spreading among our people of the immoral cult of Shabbatai Tz'vi, prince of the adulterers, which seeks the destruction of souls together with their bodies by their belief that they will bring the Messiah through the impure rites of random, indiscriminatory sex. . . . (Note: Shabbatai Tz'vi [seventeenth century] was an eccentric Turkish kabbalist who declared himself the Messiah and misled hundreds of thousands of Jews with false hopes and promises following a series of tragic pogroms in Eastern Europe that wiped out entire Jewish communities. He and his close disciples engaged in indiscriminate sexual activity, which he believed was a means of redeeming the severe impurity into which the world had fallen. He was eventually arrested by the Sultan of Turkey and converted to Islam under pain of death, though he continued living secretly as a Jew. When he was found out, he was banished to Albania. His sect continued thriving in secret for awhile after his death, ostracized by the mainstream Jewish rabbinate and their communities.]

. . . And although I am certain that nothing harmful will result from what goes forth from under my hand, as it is taught about those who strive for the benefit of the community that sin eludes them (Babylonian Talmud, *Pesachim* 8a). . . .

—for indeed all my efforts and all my writings have been with the intention of benefiting the Jewish people and promoting harmony between them and their Father in Heaven, and I have sacrificed my soul and cast to the wind my life and all of my finances for the good of my people and for their refinement and for them to regain their full authenticity in this world and the next. And in spite of my own efforts, the faith of our people would have departed nevertheless from their lips had it not been for the fact that God has been with us—

. . . nonetheless, I do not want that a person should rely exclusively on my opinion about this subject, unless it is endorsed by the Greats of the Generation. And if [my opinion] finds favor in their eyes, may my share in all this be with them and may I be like the borrower in relationship to them, borrowing of their *mitzvah*, for I am but a subsidiary to these lions, for Yaakov, who is called also *Ya'avetz* (Yaakov Emden ben Tz'vi), is small and lowly.

Furthermore, I declare to anyone who wants

to rely upon my ruling on this matter that they should first seek the involvement of a rabbinic authority, someone who is a righteous teacher and *halakhic* decisor for his community, that [this teacher] should arrange [the *pilagshut* on his behalf so that it is certain to be in such a way] that it is permissible and clean of any hurdles, that there be an exclusive relationship. This means that the woman must be accorded a private room that is hers, and he must caution her against unchaperoned liaisons with other men, and that if she is found with other men, she will be evicted from his house instantly. And he must also instruct her to perform [the postmenstrual ritual of] immersion, and he must inform her that there is no cause whatsoever for her to be embarrassed to do so [on account of not being married]. And he must also tell her that any children born from their union are considered as legitimate as any other child of Jewish descent, providing that she keeps her part of this covenant and remains faithful to this man, whereas if she has sexual relations with another man during the course of this relationship the children will be considered like the offspring of prostitutes [, concerning which there exists no stigma in Jewish law,] and anyone who has sexual relations with her from then on will be liable [for the transgression of] "There shall not be a prostitute from among the daughters of Israel" (Deut. 23:18) for every act of intercourse with her, whether it is this man or another.

In this manner, if the couple will adhere to all that has been said above, then there will be no burden of guilt or sin to bear whatsoever in this regard. On the contrary, it will be considered a *mitzvah*, one of removing obstacles that do indeed lead to sinfulness. Even more so do Torah scholars need [to know of] this option. For "one who is more spiritually evolved than their fellow, their lustful inclination is that much greater, too" (Babylonian Talmud, *Sukah* 52a). And it is appropriate for him to have "bread in his basket" (i.e., option) and for him to be able to bring a child into the world [with a *pilegesh*] if he is unable to do so through the woman that fell unto him by lottery (i.e., the woman who was destined to be his wife). And everything is determined by the intention of the heart (Babylonian Talmud, *Megilah* 20a), as long as a person's consciousness is directed toward the Heavens (Babylonian Talmud, *Berachot* 5b). For "the Compassionate One desires the heart" (Babylonian Talmud, *Sanhedrin* 106b) and "[God] watches over the walking of the pious" (I Sam. 2:9), so "do not be overly righteous" (Eccles. 7:16) lest you end up becoming overly wicked (Eccles. 7:17), as is evidenced by experience, both in regards to the great and to the small alike. And let this suffice. And I have already elongated on this subject matter more than necessary for those who understand and have wisdom regarding this topic. And I did this because "it is a time to do for God" (Ps. 119:126).

Index

Bible, sexuality in, 15
Bigamy, 132–134
Book of the Zohar,
    masturbation,
    59

Captive, sex with, 33
Childbirth, ritual
    immersion
    following, 138
Childlessness, 52, 93
Children, in *pilagshut,*
    79, 90, 93, 106,
    127, 141
Chisda, Rabbi, 8
Chiyya bar Ashi, Rabbi,
    37
Christianity, sexual
    ethic, 3–6
Coitus interruptus, 60,
    72–73
Compatibility *see*
    Sexual
    compatibility
Contraception, 93
Cook, Rabbi Avraham
    Yitzchak, 82

David and Bathsheba,
    24–25

Deuteronomy, Book of,
    3, 53, 114, 127,
    128, 133, 141
Divorce, 76, 77, 94
Dovid ibn Zimra, Rabbi,
    116
Drunkenness, sexual
    relations and, 77

Ecclesiastes, Book of,
    142
Ejaculation, extravaginal
    see Extravaginal
    ejaculation
Ejaculatory control, 75
Elai the Elder, Rabbi, 32
El'azar, Rabbi, 29
Eliezer, Rabbi, 60, 90,
    109, 110
Elior, Lakme Batya,
    85–86
Epistle of Holiness, 6
Eroticism, 16
Evil inclination, 16–17,
    22
Extravaginal ejaculation,
    52–53, 60, 69, 72

Fantasizing, during sex
    act, 77

sex during
    menstruation,
    84
sexuality, 25–26
yetzer hara, 18
Tam, Rabbeinu, 82
Tamar, rape of, 106,
    123
Torah
    coital positions, 70,
    71
    homosexuality, 53–54
    masturbation, 61
    onah, 40
    pilagshut, 88, 92,
    93, 102–103,
    125–142
    seduction, 115
Torah study, antidote to
    sexual
    preoccupation, 30–
    31
Tur, 91, 92
Twerski, Rabbi Z., 94
Tziniyut, 64–65, 66

Ultra-Orthodox Jews,
    physical contact
    between the sexes,
    19–20

Urination, holding penis
    during, 60

War, sexuality and
    soldiers, 33–34
Wasting of seed, 53,
    57, 60, 61, 69,
    72, 73
Wet dreams, 61
Women
    adultery, 9–11, 84–
    86
    bleeding,
    nonmenstrual,
    80
    childlessness, 93
    contraception, 93
    dignity of, 43–44
    foreplay, 74–75
    legal rights in
    marriage, 74
    lesbianism, 55–56
    menstrual law, 79–
    84, 91
    monthly cycle, 39–
    40, 79–84
    nidah, 79–84, 91
    nonmenstrual
    bleeding, 80
    nudity of, 63–69

About the Author

Gershon Winkler is the rabbi of the San Juan Valley Hebrew Congregation in Durango, Colorado, and of Har Shalom in Missoula, Montana. He has authored eight books, including four works on Jewish mysticism, philosophy and folklore, and was ordained by the late Rabbi Bentseon Bruk of Jerusalem and by Rabbi Zalman Schachter-Shalomi. His own journey of spiritual dissolution and re-emergence has brought him to a gleaning of the rich teachings from Judaism's lesser promulgated, non-mainstream ancient Hebraic and Aramaic texts. Rabbi Winkler is married with Lakme Batya Elior, and the couple resides in the Nacimiento Mountains of northwestern New Mexico where they conduct wilderness spirituality retreats together with Native American shamans.